MALAGA
TRAVE

A Comprehensive Companion to Exploring Spain's Dynamic Coastal City.

Cedric J. Stone.

COPYRIGHT

All rights reserved. No part of this publication may be reproduced, distributed, or transmitted in any form or by any means, including photocopying, recording, or other electronic or mechanical methods, without the prior written permission of the publisher, except in the case of brief quotations embodied in critical reviews and certain other non-commercial uses permitted by copyright law.

Copyright © 2025 by Cedric J. Stone.

To Get More of My Books, Kindly Scan the QR Code.

MALAGA SPAIN MAP

HOW TO SCAN QR-CODE

Open the Camera App:
Start by unlocking your smartphone or tablet. Open the default camera app on your device. This step is crucial as some devices can scan QR codes directly from the camera app.

Position the QR Code:
Hold your device steady and point the camera towards the QR code you want to scan. Ensure that the QR code is well-lit and within the frame of your camera.

Focus and Scan:
Your device's camera will automatically focus on the QR code. Wait for a moment until your device recognizes the QR code. You might see a notification or a pop-up indicating that the QR code has been detected.

Tap on the Notification:
If your device doesn't automatically recognize the QR code, you might need to tap on the screen where the QR code is visible. This action helps your device focus and scan the code.

Follow the Link or Action:
Once the QR code is successfully scanned, your device will typically display the associated information. This could be a website URL, contact information, app download link, or any other action associated with the QR code. Follow the displayed instructions or access the linked content.

By following these steps, you'll be able to easily scan QR codes using your smartphone or tablet camera. If your device doesn't support scanning QR codes directly from the camera app, you can download a QR code scanner app from your device's app store.

4 | *MALAGA TRAVEL GUIDE 2025*

5 | MALAGA TRAVEL GUIDE 2025

6 | MALAGA TRAVEL GUIDE 2025

TABLE OF CONTENTS

GRATITUDE 12

INTRODUCTION **13**

WELCOME TO MALAGA: THE HEART OF THE COSTA DEL SOL 13

WHY VISIT MALAGA IN 2025? 15

HOW TO USE THIS GUIDE 17

CHAPTER 1 ....**21**

THE BEST WAYS TO REACH MALAGA: AIRPORTS, TRAINS, AND MORE 21

EXPLORING THE CITY: PUBLIC TRANSPORT & WALKING AROUND 26

BEST TIMES TO VISIT: WEATHER AND SEASONAL HIGHLIGHTS 29

CHAPTER 2 ....**35**

WHERE TO STAY IN MÁLAGA: ACCOMMODATION FOR EVERY TRAVELER 35

LUXURY HOTELS IN THE CITY CENTER 36

COZY BOUTIQUE HOTELS AND GUESTHOUSES 43

VACATION RENTALS: YOUR HOME IN MALAGA 49

BEST NEIGHBORHOODS TO STAY: FROM THE HISTORIC CENTER TO THE BEACHES 55

CHAPTER 3 ....**63**

EXPLORING MALAGA'S HISTORY, ART AND ARCHITECTURE 63

THE ALCAZABA: A MOORISH FORTRESS WITH STUNNING VIEWS 64

PICASSO MUSEUM: CELEBRATING THE ARTIST'S BIRTHPLACE 70

GIBRALFARO CASTLE: A JOURNEY TO THE TOP FOR SCENIC VIEWS 76

MALAGA CATHEDRAL: A LANDMARK OF RENAISSANCE ARCHITECTURE 82

THE ROMAN THEATRE: DISCOVERING MALAGA'S ANCIENT PAST 88

CHAPTER 4 .... **95**

    OUTDOOR ADVENTURES AND NATURAL ESCAPES IN MALAGA 95

    95

    MALAGA'S BEACHES: PLAYA DE LA MALAGUETA AND BEYOND 96

    DAY TRIPS TO NEARBY BEACHES: NERJA, TORREMOLINOS, AND MARBELLA 103

    HIKING AND NATURE TRAILS: MONTES DE MÁLAGA NATURAL PARK 105

    WATER SPORTS: SURFING, PADDLEBOARDING, AND MORE 109

CHAPTER 5 .... **115**

    A CULINARY JOURNEY THROUGH MALAGA 115

    115

    TAPAS CULTURE: MUST-TRY DISHES AND LOCAL FAVORITES 116

    FINE DINING AND MICHELIN-STAR RESTAURANTS 123

    MALAGA'S WINE: EXPLORING LOCAL VARIETIES 130

    STREET FOOD: WHERE TO EAT LIKE A LOCAL 136

    SEAFOOD: A TASTE OF THE MEDITERRANEAN 143

CHAPTER 6 .... **151**

    MÁLAGA'S CULTURAL FESTIVALS AND TRADITIONS 151

    SEMANA SANTA (HOLY WEEK): A DEEP DIVE INTO MALAGA'S TRADITIONS 152

    FERIA DE AGOSTO: MALAGA'S SUMMER FAIR AND PARTY 160

    MALAGA FILM FESTIVAL: A CELEBRATION OF CINEMA 167

    FLAMENCO AND LIVE MUSIC: EXPERIENCE THE SOUL OF ANDALUSIA 175

CHAPTER 7 .... **183**

    EXPLORING MÁLAGA'S SHOPPING SCENE 183

    SOUVENIR SHOPPING: LOCAL CRAFTS AND PRODUCTS 184

    FASHION BOUTIQUES AND ANDALUSIAN MARKETS 190

El Corte Inglés: Spain's Iconic Department Store 196

Malaga's Best Shopping Streets and Malls 203

CHAPTER 8 211

Exploring Andalusia – Mountains, Beaches and Cultural Treasures 211

Ronda: A Majestic Mountain Town 212

Nerja: Beaches, Caves, and Picturesque Views 220

Granada and the Alhambra: A Must-See Day Trip 227

The Caminito del Rey: An Adventure for Nature Lovers 235

CHAPTER 9 243

Making the Most of Your Malaga Adventure 243

Budgeting for Your Trip: Tips for Affordable Travel 244

Safety Tips: What to Know for a Safe and Enjoyable Trip 251

Packing Tips: What to Bring for Every Season 259

Language and Cultural Etiquette in Malaga 266

CHAPTER 10 273

Eco-Friendly Travel Tips 273

Supporting Local Businesses and Communities 278

CHAPTER 11 283

Sample Itineraries for Every Traveler 283

1-Day Itinerary: A Day Full of Culture, History and Relaxation 284

3-Day Itinerary: Discovering the Best of Malaga 289

7-Day Itinerary: A Deeper Dive into Malaga and the Costa del Sol 297

3-Day Outdoor Lovers and Nature Enthusiasts Itinerary in Malaga 308

3-Day Romantic Getaway Itinerary: Discovering the Most Romantic Side of

Malaga 314

9 | MALAGA TRAVEL GUIDE 2025

5-Day Family-Friendly Itinerary: A Curated Itinerary for Traveling with Kids 321

CHAPTER 12 ....**329**

    Useful Apps, Resources and Contacts 329

    Essential Travel Apps for Malaga... 330

    Official Tourist Information and Visitor Contacts....................................... 333

    Emergency Contacts and Consular Services 335

    Local Guides and Tour Operators... 338

CONCLUSION **343**

    TRAVEL PLANNER 345

    345

11 | MALAGA TRAVEL GUIDE 2025

Gratitude

Dear Readers,

Thank you for choosing this book to guide you on your next adventure. Your interest and curiosity are greatly appreciated, and I am grateful for the chance to share the beauties of our world with you. Before you begin the adventures detailed within these pages, I'd like to express my heartfelt gratitude.

Your support means everything to me, and I am confident that this book will be a valuable companion on your journey. Whether you're planning your first vacation or returning to uncover new treasures, you'll find inspiration, practical insights, and a greater bond with the places you visit.

Enjoy every second of your journey, and may your memories be as breathtaking as the sights you will see.

Thank you for your participation in our adventure.

Introduction

Welcome to Malaga: The Heart of the Costa del Sol

Nestled along the sun-soaked **Costa del Sol**, Málaga is a destination that offers the perfect balance of history, culture, and coastal beauty. Known as the birthplace of Pablo Picasso, this Andalusian gem blends ancient traditions with a modern energy that captivates every traveler. Whether you're here to explore its rich artistic heritage, indulge in its celebrated cuisine, or simply bask in the Mediterranean sun, Málaga invites you to uncover its treasures at your own pace.

From the imposing walls of the **Alcazaba** to the bustling streets of the historic center, Málaga tells a story shaped by centuries of Moorish, Roman, and Spanish influence. The city's cultural offerings range from world-class museums like the **Museo Picasso Málaga** to the modern architectural marvel of **Centre Pompidou Málaga**. And if you need a break from history, Málaga's coastline offers golden sands, tranquil waters, and a stunning promenade perfect for leisurely strolls.

What sets Málaga apart is its accessibility. Whether you're arriving by air, rail, or sea, the city is a gateway to the wider **Costa del Sol and beyond**. Its **mild Mediterranean climate** ensures warm winters and sun-drenched summers, making it an ideal year-round destination.

Quick Facts: Geography and Key Highlights

- **Location**: Situated in southern Spain on the Mediterranean coast, Málaga is a gateway to Andalusia and the Costa del Sol.
- **Population**: Over 580,000 residents call Málaga home.
- **Time Zone**: Central European Time (CET).
- **Currency**: The Euro (€).
- **Language**: Spanish is the official language, but English is widely understood in tourist areas.

Why Visit Malaga in 2025?

Málaga has always been a destination that offers a little bit of everything—golden beaches, rich history, and a cultural scene that pulses with life. But 2025 is the year Málaga takes it to the next level, with exciting new events, experiences, and initiatives that make it the perfect time to visit. Whether you've been dreaming of this Andalusian gem or are returning to uncover more of its treasures, Málaga in 2025 promises unforgettable moments.

This year, Málaga will host its **first-ever Málaga Gastronomy Festival**, running from May 10 to May 20. The festival will celebrate the region's culinary heritage with pop-up markets, cooking workshops led by Michelin-starred chefs, and immersive wine-tasting experiences. A new **"Flavors of the Costa del Sol"** pavilion will showcase local ingredients, from the freshest seafood to the region's famous olives, providing a delicious introduction to Andalusian cuisine.

Nature lovers will delight in Málaga's **Sustainable Travel Initiative 2025**, which brings newly developed hiking trails to the **Montes de Málaga Natural Park**. These trails include eco-friendly facilities and guided tours focused on the region's unique biodiversity, offering a chance to connect with Málaga's natural beauty while contributing to its preservation.

Summer in Málaga also brings an expanded **Feria de Agosto (August Fair)**, running from August 10 to August 18, 2025. This iconic celebration will feature a newly **designed "Cultural Corridor"** with flamenco performances, interactive exhibits on Málaga's history, and workshops where visitors can learn traditional Andalusian crafts.

And let's not forget the coast. Málaga's port is unveiling a brand-new **Maritime Adventure Hub**, offering activities like paddleboarding, eco-diving, and electric boat tours. Whether you want to relax or seek adventure, Málaga's Mediterranean waters are yours to explore.

Lastly, Málaga's coastline is embracing its natural beauty with expanded **water sports hubs** at **Playa del Palo** and **La Malagueta**. Families can try paddleboarding, while adventurers can dive into marine life conservation experiences.

With its rich cultural offerings, upgraded natural spaces, and a timeless warmth that welcomes every traveler, Málaga in 2025 is more than a destination—it's an experience waiting to transform you. *Málaga is ready—are you?*

How to Use This Guide

This guide is your ultimate companion for exploring Málaga and its surrounding treasures. Whether you're visiting for the first time or returning to uncover new experiences, the guide is designed to offer practical advice, inspiration, and detailed information to make your trip as seamless and enriching as possible. With carefully curated sections and itineraries, it caters to every type of traveler—families, couples, history lovers, food enthusiasts, and adventurers alike.

The table of contents is your roadmap. Each chapter focuses on a specific aspect of Málaga, allowing you to easily navigate to the sections most relevant to your trip. Begin with the **Introduction** section, where you'll gain an overview of the city's essence, key highlights, and why 2025 is a special year to visit. This section sets the tone for your journey, offering insight into Málaga's history, culture, and what makes it a must-see destination.

Chapter 1 provides everything you need to know about **getting to Málaga** and **getting around** once you arrive. From transportation options to tips on walking through the city's historic streets, this chapter ensures you'll navigate Málaga with ease. You'll also find advice on the best times to visit based on weather, festivals, and local events.

If you're deciding where to stay, **Chapter 2** offers detailed recommendations across various budgets and travel styles. From **luxury hotels** to **boutique guesthouses and vacation rentals**, you'll find accommodations tailored to your preferences.

For travelers eager to dive into Málaga's rich culture, **Chapters 3 and 6** are must-reads. They explore the city's **history, art, and architecture**, along with its **festivals and traditions**, helping you understand the heart and soul of Málaga.

Outdoor enthusiasts will find inspiration in **Chapter 4**, which covers **beaches, hiking trails**, and **water sports**, while **Chapter 5** takes you on a culinary journey through Málaga's **tapas culture, fine dining**, and iconic seafood dishes.

If shopping is on your itinerary, **Chapter 7** highlights the best spots for **local crafts, fashion, and markets**. And for travelers looking to explore beyond the city, **Chapter 8** showcases incredible day trips to **Ronda, Nerja**, and the legendary **Caminito del Rey**.

Chapter 9 offers practical advice for travelers, including **budgeting tips, safety guidelines, and packing suggestions**, while **Chapter 10** emphasizes eco-friendly travel and supporting local communities.

Finally, explore the **Sample Itineraries in Chapter 11**, tailored for different interests and trip durations. Whether you're planning a quick getaway or a week-long stay, these itineraries provide structure while leaving room for personal discovery.

This guide is designed to be your trusted companion, whether you're planning your trip from home or using it to explore Málaga on the go. *Simply flip to the section that aligns with your interests, and let the adventure begin.* **Your journey begins here!**

20 | MALAGA TRAVEL GUIDE 2025

Chapter 1

The Best Ways to Reach Malaga: Airports, Trains, and More

Málaga is one of Spain's most exciting destinations, offering a mix of sun-soaked beaches, historic landmarks, and a lively cultural scene. Whether you're flying in, arriving by train, or driving, there are plenty of ways to reach this beautiful city. Once you're here, getting around is just as easy, with a well-connected public transport system and walkable streets that make exploring a breeze.

By Air: Málaga-Costa del Sol Airport (AGP)

The **Málaga-Costa del Sol Airport** (AGP) is the **main international gateway** to the city. It's the fourth busiest airport in Spain and serves flights from all over Europe and beyond. Many budget airlines, including **Ryanair, Vueling, and easyJet**, offer direct flights to Málaga, making it an affordable destination for travelers.

⌖ **Address:** Av. del Comandante García Morato, s/n, 29004 Málaga, Spain.

📞 **Contact:** +34 913 21 10 00.

🌐 **Website:** https://www.aena.es/es/malaga-costa-del-sol

Once you land, you have multiple options to reach the city center:

- **Train:** The **Cercanías C1 line** runs every 20 minutes and takes just **12 minutes** to reach **Málaga Centro-Alameda** station.

- **Bus:** The **A Express Line** (€4) runs **every 25-30 minutes** and takes **around 15 minutes** to the city center.

- **Taxi:** A taxi from the airport to the center costs around **€20-25** and takes about **15 minutes**.

- **Car Rental:** Companies like **Hertz, Europcar, and Sixt** operate at the airport.

By Train: Málaga María Zambrano Station

If you're traveling from **Madrid, Barcelona, or Seville**, taking the **AVE high-speed train** is one of the best ways to reach Málaga. The journey from **Madrid** takes around **2 hours 30 minutes**, while from **Seville**, it's just **under 2 hours**. The trains are comfortable, fast, and often include Wi-Fi.

📍 **Address:** Explanada de la Estación, 29002 Málaga, Spain.

📞 **Contact:** +34 912 320 320 (Renfe Customer Service).

🌐 **Website:** www.renfe.com

From the train station, you can reach the city center by:

- **Metro:** The **L1 and L2 metro lines** connect the station to key parts of the city.
- **Bus:** Several EMT buses stop right outside.
- **Taxi:** A taxi to the historic center costs around **€10-12**.

By Bus: Affordable & Convenient

For budget travelers, long-distance buses provide a **cheaper alternative** to trains. Companies like **ALSA and Avanza** run daily services from cities like **Granada, Madrid, and Valencia** to Málaga's main **bus station**.

⚲ **Address:** Paseo de los Tilos, s/n, 29006 Málaga, Spain.

📞 **Contact:** +34 952 35 00 51 (ALSA).

🌐 **Website:** www.alsa.es

Buses from Madrid take around **6 hours**, while from Seville, the journey is **2 hours 30 minutes**.

By Car: Road Trip to Málaga

If you prefer to drive, Málaga is well-connected by **Spain's highway network**.

- From **Madrid**: Take the **A-4 and A-45 highways** (~5 hours drive).

- From **Seville**: Take the **A-92 highway** (~2 hours 30 minutes).

- From **Granada**: The **A-92 and A-45 highways** make it a **90-minute drive**.

Parking in the city center can be difficult, so it's best to book accommodation with **private parking** or use public parking garages like:

- **Parking Plaza de la Marina** (€2 per hour, 24/7)
    - **Address:** Pl. de la Marina, 5, 29001 Málaga, Spain.
    - **Contact:** +34 952 22 23 85.

- **Parking Alcazaba** (Ideal for sightseeing)
    - **Address:** Calle Guillén Sotelo, 29015 Málaga, Spain.
    - **Contact:** +34 952 06 24 24.

Exploring the City: Public Transport & Walking Around

Málaga's Public Transport System

Málaga has a **reliable and affordable** public transport system. If you don't plan to rent a car, you can easily get around by **bus, metro, and taxis**.

1. Bus (EMT Málaga)

Málaga's local buses cover **all major tourist areas** and residential neighborhoods. Tickets cost **€1.40 per ride**, or you can buy a **10-trip card** for **€8.30**.

📍 **Main Bus Terminal:** Paseo de los Tilos, s/n, 29006 Málaga, Spain.

📞 **Contact:** +34 952 35 00 61.

🌐 **Website:** www.emtmalaga.es

2. Metro Málaga

Málaga's **metro system** is small but efficient, with just **two lines (L1 & L2)** that connect key areas like the train station and the University. A single ticket costs **€1.35**, while a day pass is **€4.50**.

📍 **Main Station:** El Perchel Metro Station.

📞 **Contact:** +34 902 11 22 22.

🌐 **Website:** www.metromalaga.es

3. Taxis & Rideshares

Taxis are **plentiful** and relatively affordable in Málaga. Some taxi companies include:

- **Unitaxi Málaga**

    📞 **Contact:** +34 952 33 33 33.

    🌐 **Website:** www.unitaxi.es.

- **Taxis en Malaga**

    📞 **Contact:** +34 665 82 78 14.

    🌐 **Website:** https://taxisenmalaga.com/

Uber and **Cabify** also operate in Málaga, offering a convenient alternative to taxis.

Walking & Bike Rentals: The Best Way to Explore

Málaga is a **very walkable city**, especially in the **historic center** where most attractions are located. The streets are pedestrian-friendly, and walking is often the best way to soak in the city's charm.

If you prefer cycling, Málaga has an **extensive bike lane network**. You can rent bikes at:

Bike Tours Malaga

- 📍 **Address:** Plaza Poeta Alfonso Canales, 4, Distrito Centro, 29001 Málaga.
- 📞 **Contact:** +34 650 67 70 63.
- 🌐 **Website:** https://www.biketoursmalaga.com/

Bike2malaga

- 📍 **Address:** C. Hoyo de Esparteros, 9, Distrito Centro, 29005 Málaga.
- 📞 **Contact:** +34 634 57 89 95.
- 🌐 **Website:** https://www.bike2malaga.com/

Tip: Málaga also has a **public bike-sharing service** called **Málagabici** (€0.50 per 30 minutes). You'll need to register at a local office before using it.

Getting to Málaga is **easy and convenient**, whether you're flying, taking a train, or arriving by bus or car. Once you're here, you'll find **plenty of ways to explore**, from walking around the charming streets to using the city's efficient public transport. In the next chapter, we'll dive into **the best places to stay in Málaga**, from budget-friendly hostels to luxury beachfront hotels!

Best Times to Visit: Weather and Seasonal Highlights

Málaga is a fantastic destination all year round, thanks to its **warm Mediterranean climate, stunning coastline, and lively cultural scene**. Whether you prefer sunny beach days, festive city vibes, or a quieter getaway, there's a perfect time to visit. Here's a breakdown of the seasons, weather, and the best times to explore Málaga based on your travel style.

Spring (March - May): Ideal for Exploring & Sightseeing

Spring is one of the **best times to visit Málaga**, with **pleasant temperatures, fewer tourists, and colorful landscapes**. The city is alive with blooming flowers, outdoor cafés, and local festivals. It's perfect for **walking tours, hiking, and sightseeing**, as the weather is warm but not too hot.

In March, temperatures hover around **18°C (64°F)**, with occasional rain. By April, it warms up to around **20°C (68°F)**, and in May, the sun shines consistently with temperatures reaching **25°C (77°F)**—great for early beachgoers.

One of the biggest highlights of spring is **Semana Santa (Holy Week), celebrated in March or April**. Málaga hosts some of Spain's **most spectacular religious processions**, drawing visitors from around the world. The streets fill with **ornate floats, music, and candlelit parades**—a truly unforgettable experience.

For those who enjoy quieter beaches, **Playa de la Malagueta** is already welcoming visitors in May, though the water might still be a bit cool. If you love outdoor adventures, spring is also a **great time for hiking in Montes de Málaga** before the summer heat kicks in.

Summer (June - August): Beach Life, Festivals & Party Atmosphere

If you're coming for the **beaches, nightlife, and festivals**, summer is the time to visit Málaga. However, it's also the **hottest and busiest season**, with peak tourism bringing **higher hotel prices and crowded attractions**.

June is still manageable, with temperatures around **28°C (82°F)**. By July and August, the heat can climb to **35°C (95°F) or more**, and humidity makes it feel even hotter. It's the perfect time to **spend your days at the beach, enjoy long seafood lunches, and stay out late exploring Málaga's famous nightlife**.

One of the city's biggest annual events is the **Feria de Málaga in August**—a **week-long celebration filled with flamenco** music, traditional food, fireworks, and parties that last until sunrise. If you enjoy a lively atmosphere, this is an incredible time to visit.

For beach lovers, **Playa de la Misericordia** is a great alternative to the more crowded Malagueta Beach. The Mediterranean waters are warm and perfect for swimming, while beachfront bars (**chiringuitos**) serve fresh seafood and cold drinks all day.

If you're planning a summer trip, make sure to **book accommodations early**, as hotels fill up fast. Also, plan activities in the morning or late afternoon to avoid the peak heat.

Autumn (September - November): Fewer Crowds, Perfect Weather & Wine Season

Autumn in Málaga offers the **best of both worlds—warm temperatures, fewer tourists, and a more relaxed atmosphere**. The summer heat lingers into September, with temperatures around **28°C (82°F)**, making it still **a great time for the beach**. By October, temperatures cool slightly to around **24°C (75°F)**, and November sees comfortable highs of **20°C (68°F)**.

This season is perfect for **exploring the city's historic sites, enjoying outdoor cafés, and even taking day trips to nearby** towns like **Ronda or Granada**. Autumn is also a fantastic time for **wine lovers**, as September and October mark the **grape harvest season** in the Málaga region. Many local wineries offer **wine-tasting experiences** during this time.

For food lovers, October is also home to the **Día del Boquerón Victoriano**, a festival dedicated to Málaga's beloved **boquerones (fried anchovies)**. If you love seafood, this is a must-visit event!

For a peaceful beach day in autumn, **Playa del Peñón del Cuervo** is a great option. With fewer tourists around, it's a perfect place to relax and enjoy the scenery.

Winter (December - February): Budget Travel & Cultural Events

Winter in Málaga is **mild compared to most of Europe**, making it a great option for travelers looking to escape the cold. **Daytime temperatures range between 12-20°C (54-68°F), and rain is occasional but not constant**. While it's not ideal for sunbathing, it's a fantastic time for **budget travelers** and those interested in culture, museums, and local traditions.

One of the best reasons to visit Málaga in winter is **its magical Christmas lights**. Calle Larios, the city's main shopping street, is **transformed into a dazzling spectacle of lights and**

decorations from early December until early January. This is one of Spain's most famous holiday light displays.

January is the **quietest month for tourism**, meaning you'll get **cheaper hotel rates and fewer crowds at major attractions like the Alcazaba, Gibralfaro Castle, and Picasso Museum**. February marks the beginning of early spring, with slightly warmer temperatures and the first signs of flowers blooming.

If you're visiting in winter, be sure to experience **Día de los Reyes Magos on January 5th**, when the city hosts a grand parade celebrating the arrival of the Three Kings—Spain's version of Christmas gift-giving.

For a relaxing winter stroll, **Playa de la Caleta** is a good spot. While it won't be warm enough for swimming, the coastal views and fresh sea breeze make for a refreshing experience.

When Should You Visit Málaga?

- If you want **warm but comfortable weather with fewer tourists**, visit in **March-May or September-October**.

- If you're coming for **beaches, nightlife, and festivals, June-August** is your season, but be ready for **crowds and high temperatures**.

- If you're looking for **budget-friendly travel and cultural experiences, November-February** is a great choice.

No matter when you visit, Málaga has something special to offer—**from sun-soaked beaches and lively festivals to rich history and world-class food**. Choose the season that matches your travel style, and get ready to enjoy this beautiful Spanish city!

Chapter 2

Where to Stay in Málaga: Accommodation for Every Traveler

Málaga offers a wide range of accommodations to suit every traveler's needs, from luxurious hotels in the heart of the city to cozy boutique guesthouses and vacation rentals by the sea. Whether you prefer staying close to the vibrant historic center or soaking up the sun near the beaches, Málaga's neighborhoods provide diverse options for every type of visitor. In this chapter, we'll guide you through the best places to stay, highlight unique lodging experiences, and help you find the perfect base for your Málaga adventure.

Luxury Hotels in the City Center

Málaga is home to some of **Spain's finest luxury hotels**, offering a mix of **historic elegance, modern comfort, and stunning views**. If you're looking for a **high-end stay in the heart of the city**, you'll find several **five-star hotels** that provide **top-tier service, rooftop pools, gourmet dining, and easy access to Málaga's best attractions**.

Below, we've listed some of the **best luxury hotels in Málaga's city center**, along with their **detailed addresses, contact information, and standout features**.

1. Gran Hotel Miramar GL – Classic Elegance with Stunning Sea Views

If you're looking for a **truly luxurious stay**, **Gran Hotel Miramar GL** is Málaga's most **iconic five-star hotel**. Set in a **beautifully restored 20th-century palace**, this hotel offers **breathtaking Mediterranean views, a rooftop terrace, a world-class spa, and Michelin-star dining**. The rooms are elegantly designed, and the location is perfect—just steps away from **La Malagueta Beach and Málaga's historic old town**.

- **Address:** Paseo Reding, 22-24, 29016 Málaga, Spain.
- **Phone:** +34 952 603 000.
- **Email:** reservas@granhotelmiramarmalaga.com
- **Website:** www.granhotelmiramarmalaga.com
- **Price Range:** Approximately **€350 to €600** per night, depending on the season and room type.

Why Stay Here?
✔ Prime location by the beach
✔ Rooftop pool with panoramic sea views
✔ Full-service spa with luxury treatments
✔ Gourmet restaurants & elegant cocktail bars

2. Vincci Selección Posada del Patio – A Stylish Five-Star Retreat

Located in the heart of Málaga, **Vincci Selección Posada del Patio** is a **modern five-star hotel** with a **sophisticated atmosphere**. What makes it unique? It's **built over an ancient Arabic wall**, which you can see inside the hotel! The rooms are **spacious and stylish**, and the **rooftop pool offers fantastic city views**. It's perfect if you want **luxury with a mix of history and modern comfort**.

- **Address:** Pasillo de Santa Isabel, 7, 29005 Málaga, Spain.
- **Phone:** +34 951 001 020.
- **Email:** posadadelpatio@vinccihoteles.com
- **Website:** www.vinccihoteles.com
- **Price Range:** Approximately €200 to €350 per night.

Why Stay Here?
✔ Rooftop swimming pool with city views.
✔ Located near Málaga's historic center.
✔ Unique historical features, including ancient ruins.
✔ Luxurious yet modern design.

3. Palacio Solecio – A Boutique Luxury Hotel in a Historic Palace

For travelers who love **classic charm with modern luxury**, **Palacio Solecio** is the perfect choice. Set in a **beautifully restored 18th-century Andalusian palace**, this boutique hotel combines **traditional Spanish architecture with five-star amenities**. It's located in the **heart of Málaga's Old Town**, just steps away from the **Picasso Museum and the Cathedral**.

- **Address:** Calle Granada, 61, 29015 Málaga, Spain.
- **Phone:** +34 952 222 000.
- **Email:** info@palaciosolecio.com
- **Website:** www.palaciosolecio.com
- **Price Range:** Approximately €200 – €450 per night.

Why Stay Here?
✔ Stunning historic architecture with modern luxury.
✔ Michelin-star restaurant on-site.
✔ Walking distance to major attractions.
✔ Personalized service & elegant atmosphere.

4. Only YOU Hotel Málaga – Trendy & Chic with a Rooftop Pool

If you're looking for **a stylish, modern hotel with a trendy vibe, Only YOU Hotel Málaga** is a fantastic option. Located right by the **Port of Málaga**, it offers **breathtaking sea views, a rooftop pool, and sleek contemporary rooms**. This hotel is perfect for **luxury travelers who love a mix of fashion, design, and great service**.

- **Address:** Alameda Principal, 1, 29001 Málaga, Spain.
- **Phone:** +34 951 39 00 69.
- **Email:** info@onlyyouhotels.com
- **Website:** www.onlyyouhotels.com
- **Price Range:** Approximately €350 – €500 per night.

Why Stay Here?

✔ Rooftop pool with amazing views.
✔ Ultra-modern design with a stylish atmosphere.
✔ Located near Málaga's port & shopping areas.
✔ Perfect for couples & luxury travelers.

5. Hotel Molina Lario – A Sophisticated Stay in the Heart of Malaga

Hotel Molina Lario is a **four-star superior hotel** that feels like a **five-star stay**, thanks to its **impeccable service, luxurious rooms, and fantastic location**. Overlooking the **Málaga Cathedral**, it offers **a rooftop terrace with breathtaking city views**, a stylish bar, and a **relaxing outdoor pool**.

- **Address:** Calle Molina Lario, 20, 29015 Málaga, Spain.
- **Phone:** +34 952 062 002.
- **Email:** info@molinolario.com
- **Website:** https://www.hotelmolinalario.com/
- **Price Range:** Approximately €180 to €250 per night.

Why Stay Here?

✔ Prime location next to Málaga Cathedral.
✔ Rooftop pool with city views.
✔ Elegant yet relaxed atmosphere.
✔ Perfect for a luxurious city break.

Which Luxury Hotel is Right for You?

- For beachfront luxury with five-star elegance: Gran Hotel Miramar GL.
- For a mix of modern comfort and history: Vincci. Selección Posada del Patio
- For a boutique hotel with classic charm: Palacio Solecio
- For trendy travelers who love stylish stays: Only YOU Hotel Málaga
- For a sophisticated city-center hotel with great views: Hotel Molina Lario

No matter which luxury hotel you choose, you'll be staying in **one of the best locations in Málaga,** surrounded by the city's top attractions, beaches, and dining spots.

Cozy Boutique Hotels and Guesthouses

If you prefer a **charming, intimate stay** over a large luxury hotel, Málaga has plenty of **cozy boutique hotels and guesthouses** that offer **a warm atmosphere, personalized service, and unique design**. Whether you're looking for **a stylish boutique hotel in the city center, a charming Andalusian guesthouse, or a quiet retreat with a homey feel**, you'll find something special in Málaga.

Here are some of the **best boutique hotels and guesthouses**, along with their **contact details, addresses, and what makes them unique**.

1. Hotel Boutique Teatro Romano – Stay in the Heart of History

For travelers who love **history, culture, and boutique charm**, **Hotel Boutique Teatro Romano** is a fantastic choice. This **small, stylish hotel** is located **right in front of the Roman Theatre and Alcazaba**, offering some of the **best views in Málaga**. The rooms are **modern yet cozy**, and the location is perfect for **exploring Málaga's Old Town, museums, and tapas bars**.

- **Address:** Calle Alcazabilla, 7, 29015 Málaga, Spain.

- **Phone:** +34 951 20 44 38.

- **Email:** info@hotelbouteatro.com

- **Website:** https://hotelteatroromano.com/
- **Price Range:** Approximately €90 to €120 per night.

Why Stay Here?

✔ **Unbeatable location** in Málaga's historic center.

✔ Cozy rooms with **modern design and historic views.**

✔ Surrounded by some of Málaga's **best tapas bars and cafés.**

✔ **Great value** for a boutique stay.

2. Anahita Boutique Hotel – Stylish and Elegant Stay

Set in a **beautifully restored 18th-century building, Anahita Boutique Hotel** is **a mix of traditional Andalusian charm and modern elegance**. The hotel features **spacious rooms, a rooftop terrace, and a cozy café**, making it ideal for a **relaxing stay** in Málaga's city center.

- **Address:** C. Álamos, 41, Distrito Centro, 29012 Málaga.

- **Phone:** +34 952 00 92 53.

- **Email:** info@anahitaboutiquehotel.com

- **Website:** https://www.hotelanahita.com/
- **Price Range:** Approximately €75 to €110.

Why Stay Here?

✔ Elegant **historic architecture with modern comfort.**

✔ **Quiet and peaceful atmosphere** in the city center.

✔ Rooftop terrace with **lovely city views.**

✔ **Excellent breakfast and friendly staff.**

3. Madeinterranea Suites – A Hidden Gem with a Homey Feel

For travelers who love **small, family-run guesthouses with a personal touch**, **Madeinterranea Suites** is an excellent choice. This **cozy boutique hotel** has just a few rooms, making it **intimate and peaceful**. The décor is **stylish and minimalist**, with a mix of **modern design and natural materials**.

- **Address:** C. Andrés Pérez, 5, Distrito Centro, 29008 Málaga.
- **Phone:** +34 952 91 68 01.
- **Email:** reservas@madeinterranea.com
- **Website:** https://madeinterranea.es/

- **Price Range:** Approximately €85 to €120.

Why Stay Here?

✔ **Feels like a home away from home.**

✔ Cozy, **minimalist rooms with a warm atmosphere.**

✔ Delicious **homemade breakfast included.**

✔ **Great value** for a boutique hotel.

4. Hotel Casa de las Mercedes – A Traditional Andalusian Guesthouse

If you want to **experience Málaga like a local**, **Casa de las Mercedes** is a **beautiful, family-run guesthouse** with a **traditional Andalusian feel**. The building is a **historic 18th-century house**, decorated with **colorful tiles, wooden beams, and vintage furniture**. The owners are **incredibly welcoming**, making you feel like you're staying at a **friend's home**.

- **Address:** Calle Hinestrosa, 18, 29012 Málaga, Spain.

- **Phone:** +34 951 24 39 13.

- **Email:** info@casadelasmercedes.com

- **Website:** https://www.casadelamercedsuites.com/

- **Price Range:** Approximately €80 to €120 per night.

Why Stay Here?

✔ **Authentic Andalusian charm** with a cozy feel.

✔ **Family-run guesthouse with friendly hosts.**

✔ **Beautiful, historic décor.**

✔ Located in a **quiet, picturesque street.**

5. La Casa Azul – A Cozy Bed & Breakfast by the Beach

For travelers who want to **stay near the beach**, La Casa Azul B&B is a fantastic **boutique guesthouse.** This small **bed & breakfast** is located **just a short walk from La Malagueta Beach**, offering a **relaxed, coastal vibe.** The rooms are **bright, colorful, and charming**, and the **homemade breakfast is a highlight.**

- **Address:** Avenida de Príes, 20, 29016 Málaga, Spain.
- **Phone:** +34 951 95 66 21.
- **Email:** info@lacasazulbb.com
- **Website:** https://www.lacasaazulmalaga.com/
- **Price Range:** Approximately €10 to €150 per night.

Why Stay Here?

✔ **Perfect for beach lovers** – just minutes from **La**

Malagueta Beach.

✔ Cozy, colorful rooms with a Mediterranean vibe.

✔ Homemade breakfast with fresh, local ingredients.

✔ Located in a **quiet, residential area.**

Which Boutique Stay is Best for You?

○ **For history lovers who want a stay in the Old Town:** Hotel Boutique Teatro Romano.

○ **For a stylish, elegant boutique experience:** Anahita Boutique Hotel.

○ **For a small, intimate guesthouse with a personal feel:** Madeinterranea Suites.

○ **For a traditional Andalusian-style guesthouse:** Casa de las Mercedes.

○ **For a cozy beachside stay with a relaxed atmosphere:** La Casa Azul B&B.

Each of these boutique hotels and guesthouses **offers something unique**, whether it's **a historic location, a cozy homey feel, or a stylish design.** If you want a **more personal and intimate experience** than a large hotel, **these are the best places to stay in Málaga.**

Vacation Rentals: Your Home in Malaga

Vacation Rentals: Your Home in Málaga

If you're looking for a **comfortable, home-like stay in Málaga**, vacation rentals are a great option. Whether you want **a stylish apartment in the city center, a beachfront villa, or a quiet house in a charming neighborhood**, Málaga has plenty of options to choose from. **Vacation rentals give you more space, privacy, and flexibility**, making them a perfect choice for **families, groups, couples, or solo travelers who want a more relaxed and independent stay.**

Here are some of the **best vacation rentals in Málaga**, along with their **contact details, addresses, and what makes them special**.

1. Feelathome Merced Apartments – Modern Stays in the Historic Center

Located **just steps from Plaza de la Merced**, Feelathome Merced Apartments offer **modern, fully equipped apartments** in the heart of Málaga. The apartments are **stylish, spacious, and perfect for travelers who want to explore the city on foot.** Each unit has **a fully equipped kitchen, a comfortable living area, and air conditioning**.

- **Address:** Calle Medina Conde, 3, 29015 Málaga, Spain.

- **Phone:** +34 659 14 09 21.

- **Email:** info@feelathome.com

- **Website:** www.feelathome.com

- **Price Range:** Approximately €70 to €120 per night.

Why Stay Here?

✔ **Great location in the Old Town.**

✔ **Modern and fully equipped apartments.**

✔ **Perfect for long or short stays.**

✔ **Walking distance to restaurants, museums, and attractions.**

2. Living4Malaga Skyline Apartments – Sea Views & Luxury

For travelers who want **stunning sea views and modern comfort**, Living4Malaga Skyline Apartments is a fantastic choice. These **high-end apartments are located near La Malagueta Beach**, offering **beautiful terraces with panoramic views of the Mediterranean.**

- **Address:** Calle Paseo Marítimo Ciudad de Melilla, 29016 Málaga, Spain.

- **Email:** reservas@living4malaga.com

- **Website:** www.living4malaga.com

- **Price Range:** Approximately €80 to €150 per night.

Why Stay Here?

✔ Beachfront location with stunning sea views.

✔ Luxury apartments with modern décor.

✔ Private terraces and spacious rooms.

✔ Great for couples or families.

3. Casa de la Merced Suites – A Charming Andalusian Stay

For travelers who love **authentic charm and boutique-style rentals**, Casa de la Merced Suites is a **beautiful vacation rental set in a restored historic building**. It offers **charming, cozy apartments** with **traditional Andalusian décor and a peaceful atmosphere**.

- **Address:** C. Granada, 82, Distrito Centro, 29015 Málaga.

- **Phone:** +34 952 21 76 35.

- **Email:** info@casadelamercedsuites.com

- **Website:** www.casadelamercedsuites.com

51 | MALAGA TRAVEL GUIDE 2025

- **Price Range:** Approximately €80 to €120 per night.

Why Stay Here?

✔ Authentic Andalusian charm with modern comfort.

✔ Located in a lively plaza with great restaurants nearby.

✔ Perfect for couples and solo travelers.

✔ Feels like a boutique hotel but with home-like privacy.

4. Málaga Center Flat Holidays – Family-Friendly Apartments

If you're traveling with **family or a group**, Málaga Center Flat Holidays offers **spacious vacation rentals with multiple bedrooms, large living spaces, and fully equipped kitchens**. These rentals are **located in different areas of Málaga**, from the historic center to the beachside.

- **Address:** C. Mármoles, 30, Distrito Centro, 29007 Málaga, Spain.

- **Phone:** +34 951 10 03 33.

- **Email:** info@malagacenterflat.com

- **Website:** https://malagacenterflat.com/

- **Price Range:** Approximately **€50 to €100** per night.

Why Stay Here?

✔ **Large apartments ideal for families and groups.**

✔ **Great locations close to attractions and public transport.**

✔ **Full kitchens and laundry facilities for longer stays.**

✔ **Affordable pricing for big groups.**

5. Apartamentos Nono – Stylish Apartments in Soho Málaga

For travelers who love **trendy neighborhoods and a modern atmosphere**, Apartamentos Nono is an **amazing vacation rental in the heart of Soho Málaga**. The apartments are **chic, well-designed, and offer a stylish home-away-from-home experience**.

- **Address:** Calle Casas de Campos, 15, 29001 Málaga, Spain.
- **Phone:** +34 951 35 91 07.
- **Email:** reservas@apartamentosnono.com
- **Website:** https://charmingstay.es/nono-apartamentos-malaga/
- **Price Range:** Approximately **€80 to €135** per night.

Why Stay Here?

✔ Trendy location in Málaga's artistic Soho district.

✔ Beautiful, modern apartments with sleek designs.

✔ Walking distance to the city center and the port.

✔ Perfect for couples or digital nomads.

Which Vacation Rental is Best for You?

🏠 for a modern, central apartment: Feelathome Merced Apartments.

🏖 For a luxurious beachfront stay: Living4Malaga. Skyline Apartments

🌿 For a charming Andalusian-style stay: Casa de la Merced Suites.

👨‍👩‍👧 For family-friendly, spacious rentals: Málaga Center Holidays.

🎨 For a trendy, stylish city apartment: Apartamentos Nono in Soho Málaga.

With **so many amazing vacation rentals in Málaga**, you'll easily find the perfect place to stay **whether you're visiting for a short city break, a romantic getaway, or a long vacation.**

Best Neighborhoods to Stay: From the Historic Center to the Beaches

Málaga is a city with **a variety of neighborhoods, each offering a unique experience.** Whether you want to be **in the heart of the Old Town, near the beach, or in a trendy, artistic district**, there's a perfect place for you. Here's a **detailed guide to the best neighborhoods** to stay in Málaga, including **where to stay, what to expect, and the best accommodations with contact details.**

1. Centro Histórico – Stay in the Heart of Málaga

If you want to be **right in the middle of Málaga's history, culture, and nightlife**, the **Centro Histórico (Historic Center)** is the best place to stay. You'll be surrounded by **narrow cobblestone streets, colorful buildings, and some of the city's top attractions, like the Alcazaba, the Cathedral, and the Picasso Museum**. The area is **perfect for first-time visitors** who want to explore Málaga on foot.

Best Hotels & Vacation Rentals in Centro Histórico

📍 **Hotel Molina Lario** – A stylish boutique hotel with rooftop views.

Address: Calle Molina Lario, 20, 29015 Málaga, Spain.

- **Phone:** +34 952 062 002.

- **Email:** info@molinolario.com

- **Website:** https://www.hotelmolinalario.com/

🏠 **Feelathome Merced Apartments** – Modern, comfortable vacation rentals near Plaza de la Merced.

- **Address:** Calle Medina Conde, 3, 29015 Málaga, Spain.

- **Phone:** +34 659 14 09 21.

- **Email:** info@feelathome.com

- **Website:** www.feelathome.com

Why Stay Here?

✔ Perfect for sightseeing and exploring on foot.

✔ Great restaurants, tapas bars, and nightlife nearby.

✔ Close to all major attractions.

✔ Lively and full of energy.

2. La Malagueta – Beachfront Living with City Access

If you love the **beach but still want to be close to the city center**, **La Malagueta** is a fantastic choice. This neighborhood is just a **10-minute walk from the historic center**, yet it offers relaxing seaside vibes, golden sand beaches, and stunning views of the Mediterranean.

Best Hotels & Vacation Rentals in La Malagueta

📩 **Gran Hotel Miramar** – A luxurious beachfront hotel with top-notch service.

- **Address:** Paseo Reding 22, 29016 Málaga, Spain.
- **Phone:** +34 952 603 000.
- **Email:** info@granhotelmiramarmalaga.com
- **Website:** www.granhotelmiramarmalaga.com

🏠 **Living4Malaga Skyline Apartments** – Modern apartments with sea views.

- **Address:** Calle Paseo Marítimo Ciudad de Melilla, 29016 Málaga, Spain.
- **Email:** reservas@living4malaga.com
- **Website:** www.living4malaga.com

Why Stay Here?
✔ Best for beach lovers who still want city access.
✔ Great seafood restaurants and beachfront bars.

✔ Quieter than the historic center.

✔ Perfect for families and couples.

3. Soho Málaga – Trendy & Artistic Vibes

Soho Málaga is **Málaga's creative and artistic neighborhood**, filled with **street art, independent cafes, boutique shops, and a cool urban feel**. It's located **right next to the historic center**, making it an excellent choice for travelers who **love art, culture, and a relaxed atmosphere**.

Best Hotels & Vacation Rentals in Soho Málaga

🎨 **Only YOU Hotel Málaga** – A stylish, design-focused hotel with incredible city views.

- **Address:** Alameda Principal 1, 29001 Málaga, Spain.

- **Phone:** +34 951 39 00 69.

- **Email:** info@onlyyouhotels.com

- **Website:** www.onlyyouhotels.com

🏠 **Apartamentos Nono** – Chic, modern apartments in the heart of Soho.

- **Address:** Calle Casas de Campos, 15, 29001 Málaga, Spain.

- **Phone:** +34 951 35 91 07.

- **Email:** reservas@apartamentosnono.com
- **Website:** https://charmingstay.es/nono-apartamentos/

Why Stay Here?

✔ Trendy and artistic atmosphere.

✔ Close to the city center and the port.

✔ Cool bars, unique cafes, and boutique shopping.

✔ Great for younger travelers and digital nomads.

4. Pedregalejo – A Relaxed, Local Beach Experience

Pedregalejo is a **laid-back, beachside neighborhood with a local feel**. It's located **a bit outside the city center**, making it perfect for travelers who **want a quieter stay with an authentic, residential atmosphere**. The area is known for its **small sandy beaches, traditional seafood restaurants, and relaxed vibes**.

Best Hotels & Vacation Rentals in Pedregalejo

🐊 **La Casa Azul B&B** – A charming, colorful bed & breakfast with a homely feel.

- **Address:** Avenida de Príes 20, 29016 Málaga, Spain.
- **Phone:** +34 951 95 66 21.
- **Email:** info@lacasazulmalaga.com

- **Website:** www.lacasazulmalaga.com

🏠 **Elcano Hotel** – A cozy, budget-friendly stay near the beach.

- **Address:** Avenida Juan Sebastián Elcano 103, 29017 Málaga, Spain.
- **Phone:** +34 952 204 303.
- **Email:** info@hotelelcano.es
- **Website:** https://hotelelcanomalaga.es/
- **Price Range:** Approximately €100 to €120 per night.

Why Stay Here?

✔ Quiet, local atmosphere with a beachside feel.

✔ Great for relaxing and enjoying fresh seafood.

✔ Less touristy than other areas.

✔ Perfect for couples and solo travelers.

Which Neighborhood is Best for You?

🏛 For history lovers and first-time visitors: Centro Histórico.

🏖 For beach lovers who want city access: La Malagueta.

🎨 for a trendy, artistic vibe: Soho Málaga.

🏖 For a quiet, local beach experience: Pedregalejo.

No matter where you choose to stay, **Málaga's neighborhoods offer something unique for every traveler**. From **historic streets and sandy beaches to trendy cafes and artistic hubs**, there's a perfect place for you to call home during your trip.

61 | MALAGA TRAVEL GUIDE 2025

62 | MALAGA TRAVEL GUIDE 2025

Chapter 3

Exploring Malaga's History, Art and Architecture

Málaga is a city where **history, culture, and art** intertwine seamlessly, offering visitors a rich tapestry of experiences. From the **ancient ruins of the Roman Theatre** to the Moorish elegance of the **Alcazaba and Gibralfaro Castle**, the city is a treasure trove of landmarks that reflect its storied past. Coupled with a celebration of modern art at the **Picasso Museum** and the grandeur of the **Málaga Cathedral**, this chapter takes you on a journey through the city's most iconic sites, blending history and creativity with breathtaking views and architectural brilliance.

The Alcazaba: A Moorish Fortress with Stunning Views

Málaga's **Alcazaba** is one of **the most impressive historical sites in Spain**. This **ancient Moorish fortress**, built in the **11th century**, sits on a hill overlooking the city, offering **breathtaking panoramic views** of Málaga, the harbor, and the Mediterranean Sea. It's a place where **history, architecture, and nature come together beautifully**. If you're visiting Málaga, **this is a must-see attraction** that takes you back in time while providing some of the best photo opportunities in the city.

A Glimpse into the Past

The **Alcazaba** was built by the **Moors**, the Muslim rulers of Spain, in **the 11th century**. It was **designed as both a fortress** and a palace, similar to the famous **Alhambra in Granada**, but on a smaller scale. The location was chosen strategically to **protect the city from invaders**, with its **thick stone walls, defensive towers, and hidden pathways**. Today, it is **one of the best-preserved Moorish fortresses in Spain** and walking through it feels like stepping into another era.

Exploring the Alcazaba: What to See

Walking through the Alcazaba is like **entering a different world**. The **stone pathways, archways, and lush gardens** make for a stunning setting. Here are some of the highlights you shouldn't miss:

1. The Entrance & Outer Walls

As you **enter the Alcazaba**, you'll walk through a **series of gates and stone archways**. These were built to **confuse and slow down invaders**. The thick walls and **watchtowers** give you a sense of how well-protected this fortress was.

2. The Patio de Armas (Courtyard of Arms)

This **open courtyard** was used for military exercises. Today, it's a peaceful space with **fountains, gardens, and shaded areas** where you can take a break and admire the surroundings.

3. The Palace & Moorish Architecture

Inside the fortress, you'll find **the palace area**, where the rulers once lived. The architecture is **a beautiful mix of Moorish and Andalusian styles**, featuring **intricate arches, tiled walls, and elegant patios**. The **views from here are incredible**, especially at sunset.

4. The Tower of Homage

One of the **highest points** in the Alcazaba, this tower gives you **a 360-degree view of Málaga**. You can see the **cathedral, the port, and even the mountains in the distance**.

Best Time to Visit

 Morning or Late Afternoon – The best times to visit are **early in the morning or late in the afternoon**, as the temperatures are cooler and the lighting is perfect for photos.

 Spring & Autumn – If you visit **between March-May or September-November**, the weather is **comfortable**, and the site is **less crowded** than in the peak summer months.

Ticket Information & Opening Hours

 General Admission: €3.50.

 Combined Ticket (Alcazaba + Gibralfaro Castle): €5.50.

🎟 **Discounts:** Seniors & students – €1.50.

🎟 **Free Entry:** Every Sunday after 2:00 PM.

⏰ **Opening Hours:**

- **Winter (Nov-Mar):** 9:00 AM - 6:00 PM.
- **Summer (Apr-Oct):** 9:00 AM - 8:00 PM.

How to Get There

🚶 **Walking:** If you're staying in the **city center**, it's a **10-minute walk** from Plaza de la Merced or Calle Larios.

🚌 **Bus:** Take **bus line 35** from Alameda Principal to the entrance.

🚗 **By Car:** Parking is available at **Muelle Uno (Port Area)** or Plaza de la Marina.

Visitor Information:

📍 **Address:** Calle Alcazabilla, 2, 29012 Málaga, Spain.

📞 **Phone:** +34 951 926 051.

✉ **Email:** info@malagaturismo.com

🌐 **Website:** https://alcazabaygibralfaro.malaga.eu/

Where to Eat Nearby

After visiting the Alcazaba, **you might want to grab a bite** at one of the **fantastic restaurants nearby**. Here are two great options:

🍽 **El Pimpi** – Famous for its **traditional tapas and wine**.

- **Address:** Calle Granada, 62, 29015 Málaga, Spain.

- **Phone:** +34 952 22 54 03.

- **Email:** reservas@elpimpi.com

- **Website:** www.elpimpi.com

- **Price Range:** Approximately **€20 to €40** per person.

🍽 **La Barra de Zapata** – Small, cozy spot with **delicious Andalusian cuisine**.

- **Address:** Calle Salinas, 10, 29015 Málaga, Spain.

- **Phone:** +34 673 42 67 90.

- **Email:** info@labarradezapata.com

- **Price Range**: Approximately **€30 to €50** per person.

The **Alcazaba of Málaga is not just a historical site; it's an experience**. Whether you're interested in **history, architecture, photography, or simply enjoying a peaceful**

walk with amazing views, this fortress **has something for everyone**. It's one of the **best-preserved Moorish fortresses in Spain**, and **its strategic location gives you some of the best views in the city**.

If you're planning a trip to Málaga, **make sure the Alcazaba is at the top of your list!**

Picasso Museum: Celebrating the Artist's Birthplace

Málaga is **the birthplace of Pablo Picasso**, one of the most **influential artists in history**. If you're visiting the city, you can't miss the **Picasso Museum Málaga (Museo Picasso Málaga)**—a place that celebrates the **life and work of the legendary artist**. Located in a beautiful **16th-century palace**, the museum houses **over 200 of Picasso's original artworks**, spanning different periods of his career. Whether you're an **art lover or just curious about Picasso's genius**, this museum offers a **fascinating insight** into his creativity and legacy.

Why Visit the Picasso Museum?

🎨 **See Original Picasso Artworks** – The museum holds a **permanent collection** of Picasso's **paintings, drawings, sculptures, and ceramics**, showcasing his **evolution as an artist**.

🏛 **Historic Setting** – The museum is inside the **Palacio de Buenavista**, a **stunning Renaissance-style palace** with **Moorish influences**. Walking through the halls feels like stepping into **another era**.

📖 **Learn About Picasso's Life** – The exhibits **explore his artistic journey**, from his **early sketches** to his **most famous works**, giving visitors a **deeper understanding of his genius**.

🖼️ **Temporary Exhibitions** – In addition to the **permanent collection**, the museum regularly hosts **temporary exhibitions** featuring works by **other great artists** connected to Picasso's style.

What to See Inside the Museum

1. The Permanent Collection

The museum features **over 200 pieces of Picasso's work**, covering **his entire career**. You'll see **everything from early sketches to Cubist masterpieces**. Some highlights include:

- "Woman with Raised Arms" (1936) – A great example of Picasso's abstract style.

- "Mother and Child" (1921) – A softer, more emotional piece from his **classical period**.

- "The Three Graces" (1923) – A unique interpretation of a **traditional theme**.

2. Temporary Exhibitions

The museum often features **special exhibits** that focus on **Picasso's influences and connections to other artists** like Matisse, Miró, or Dalí.

3. The Archaeological Site

Beneath the museum, you'll find **remains of a Phoenician wall**, a reminder of Málaga's **ancient history**. It's an unexpected **bonus** that adds depth to the visit.

4. The Beautiful Courtyard & Architecture

Even if you're not a big art fan, the **Palacio de Buenavista** itself is worth visiting. The **inner courtyard, stone arches, and Andalusian-style patios** make it a **peaceful and picturesque spot** to explore.

Best Time to Visit

🕘 **Morning Visit:** Arrive **early** to avoid crowds, especially during weekends.

📅 **Weekdays Are Quieter:** If possible, visit **Monday-Thursday** for a more relaxed experience.

☺ **Spring & Autumn:** March-May and September-November are **ideal** for visiting Málaga, as the weather is pleasant, and the city isn't as crowded as in summer.

Ticket Prices & Opening Hours

🎟 **General Admission:** €12.

🎟 **Reduced Price:** €8 (students, seniors, and groups).

🎟 **Free Entry:** Every **Sunday after 4:00 PM.**

⏰ **Opening Hours:**

- **March to June:** 10:00 AM - 7:00 PM.
- **July to August:** 10:00 AM - 8:00 PM.
- **September to February:** 10:00 AM - 6:00 PM.
- **Closed on December 25th & January 1st.**

How to Get There

🚶 **Walking:** The museum is in the **historic center**, just a **5-minute walk from the Cathedral.**

🚌 **Public Transport:** Take **bus lines 1, 3, 4, 11, or 32** to Plaza de la Merced.

🚙 **By Car:** Park at **Muelle Uno or Alcazaba Parking**, both within **a 10-minute walk**.

Visitor Information:

📍 **Address:** Palacio de Buenavista, Calle San Agustín, 8, 29015 Málaga, Spain.

📞 **Phone:** +34 952 127 600.

✉️ **Email:** info@museopicassomalaga.org

🌐 **Website:** www.museopicassomalaga.org

Where to Eat Nearby

After exploring the Picasso Museum, you might want to **grab a bite** at one of these nearby spots:

🍽️ **Casa Lola** – A lively tapas bar with a great selection of **Spanish dishes and wines**.

- **Address:** Calle Granada, 46, 29015 Málaga, Spain.

- **Phone:** +34 952 22 34 14.

- **Website:** https://menu.tipsipro.com

- **Price Range:** Approximately **€10 to €20** per person

🍽️ **El Tapeo de Cervantes** – Small and cozy, known for **authentic tapas and friendly service**.

- **Address:** Calle Carcer, 8, 29012 Málaga, Spain.

- **Phone:** +34 952 609 458.

- **Website:** www.eltapeodecervantes.com

- **Price Range:** Approximately €10 to €20 per person.

🍽 **La Cosmopolita** – A mix of **modern and traditional Spanish cuisine**, great for **lunch or dinner**.

- **Address:** Calle José Denis Belgrano, 3, 29015 Málaga, Spain.

- **Phone:** +34 952 215 827.

- **Website:** www.lacosmopolita.es

- **Price Range:** Approximately €30 to €50 per person.

Even if you **aren't a big art fan**, the **Picasso Museum Málaga** is a place you **shouldn't miss**. It's a chance to see **original works by one of the greatest artists of all time**, all in a **beautifully restored palace** in the heart of Málaga. Whether you're exploring his **Cubist masterpieces** or simply enjoying the **historic surroundings**, this museum offers a **unique cultural experience**.

If you're planning to visit Málaga, make sure **this museum is on your list!**

Gibralfaro Castle: A Journey to the Top for Scenic Views

Gibralfaro Castle: A Journey to the Top for Scenic Views

If you're in Málaga and love breathtaking views, then **Gibralfaro Castle** should definitely be on your list. Standing tall on a hill overlooking the city, this **historic fortress** offers **panoramic views** of the entire city, the **Mediterranean Sea**, and even the **Malaga port**. It's one of the **best spots to enjoy a bird's-eye view of Málaga**, and the journey up is just as rewarding as the view itself.

Visiting **Gibralfaro Castle** isn't just about the views—it's about stepping back in time and experiencing a place that's been part of Málaga's history for centuries. Whether you're a history buff or just love being in high places, this castle provides an unforgettable experience.

Why Visit Gibralfaro Castle?

🏰 **A Historic Castle with Stunning Views** – The castle is a must-see for anyone who wants to enjoy some of the **best views in Málaga**.

🔒 **A Step Back in Time** – Built in the **14th century**, the castle offers a glimpse into the **past** and lets you understand the city's **military history**.

🎨 **Beautiful Walks and Photo Opportunities** – The **paths around the castle** are perfect for walking and taking stunning photos, especially with the **Mediterranean Sea** in the background.

🌿 **A Relaxing Escape** – Even though it's a popular spot for tourists, the peaceful atmosphere and scenic views make it a **great place to relax** and enjoy nature.

What You'll See at Gibralfaro Castle

1. The Stunning Views

The **main attraction** of Gibralfaro Castle is the view. From the top, you can see the **entire city of Málaga**, stretching down to the **beaches and the Mediterranean Sea**. It's especially magical at **sunset** when the sky lights up with vibrant colors.

2. The Castillo's History

The castle was built in **the 14th century** by the **Nasrid dynasty**, and it's one of the oldest military structures in Spain. It was originally used as a **watchtower** and **military base**, designed to protect the nearby **Alcazaba fortress**. The **information panels** inside the castle explain its fascinating history, from its military importance to how it was **restored** in the 20th century.

3. The Scenic Walk

The **pathway** leading up to the castle is lined with **lush trees** and offers some of the **best views** of the city along the way. It's a **pleasant 20-minute walk**, but if you're not up for the climb, there's also a **bus** that can take you up.

4. The Tower and Walls

The **castle walls** and **watchtowers** offer the perfect spots for taking pictures or just taking in the views. Don't forget to check out the **tower** at the top, where you can see **360-degree views** of Málaga and beyond.

Best Time to Visit

⏰ **Early Morning**: If you want to avoid the crowds and enjoy the calm atmosphere, try to visit in the **morning** right when it opens.

📅 **Spring and Autumn**: The best times to visit are in **spring (March-May)** or **autumn (September-November)** when the weather is **pleasant** and not too hot. Avoid the peak summer months unless you enjoy the hustle and bustle.

☺ **Sunset Views**: For the most **stunning scenery**, try to time your visit for around **sunset**, when the city is bathed in soft golden light.

Ticket Prices & Opening Hours

🎫 **General Admission**: €3.50.

🎫 **Reduced Price** (Students, seniors): €1.75.

🎫 **Free Entry**: On Sundays, entry is free after 2:00PM.

⏰ **Opening Hours**:

- **March to October**: 9:00 AM - 8:00 PM.
- **November to February**: 9:00 AM - 6:00 PM.

Visitor Information:

📍 **Address**: Camino de Gibralfaro, 11, 29016 Málaga, Spain.

📞 **Phone**: +34 952 22 72 30.

📧 **Email**: castillogibralfaro.malaga@malaga.eu

🌐 **Website**: https://alcazabaygibralfaro.malaga.eu/

How to Get There

🚶 **Walking**: If you're up for a little adventure, the **walk from the Alcazaba** to Gibralfaro Castle is only about 15 minutes and will take you **through beautiful gardens** and offer great views along the way.

🚌 **Public Transport**: Take bus **35** from the city center, which will drop you off near the entrance of the castle.

🚗 **By Car**: The best parking is around the **base of the hill**, and it's a short **walk up** to the entrance. Be sure to check for parking signs since the area can get busy.

Where to Eat Nearby

After visiting the castle, treat yourself to a meal at one of these **restaurants nearby** with great views of the city.

🍽 **El Pimpi** – A classic spot known for its **delicious tapas** and lively atmosphere.

- **Address**: Calle Granada, 62, 29015 Málaga, Spain.

- **Phone**: +34 952 22 54 03.

- **Website**: www.elpimpi.com

- **Price Range:** Approximately **€20 to €40** per person.

🍽 **Restaurante Vino Mío** – A cozy restaurant with a great selection of wines and local dishes.

- **Address**: Plaza de Jerónimo Cuervo, 2, Distrito Centro, 29012 Málaga.

- **Phone**: +34 952 60 90 33.

- **Website**: www.vinomio.es

- **Price Range:** Approximately **€15 to €40** per person.

🍽 **La Cosmopolita** – Enjoy **modern Andalusian cuisine** in a stylish yet casual setting.

- **Address**: Calle José Denis Belgrano, 3, 29015 Málaga, Spain.

- **Phone**: +34 952 215 827.

- **Website**: www.lacosmopolita.es

- **Price Range:** Approximately **€30 to €50** per person.

Gibralfaro Castle is one of those places in Málaga where you'll not only get to experience **rich history** but also get an **amazing view** of the city. Whether you're interested in history, photography, or simply love the idea of **exploring a castle**, the **Gibralfaro Castle** provides something for everyone.

So, if you're looking for **spectacular views and a touch of history**, don't miss out on this must-see spot in Málaga!

Malaga Cathedral: A Landmark of Renaissance Architecture

If you're visiting Málaga, one of the must-see landmarks is the **Malaga Cathedral**, a breathtaking example of Andalusian Renaissance architecture. Known locally as **La Manquita** (the one-armed lady) due to its unfinished south tower, this cathedral offers a fascinating glimpse into the city's rich history, architectural evolution, and artistic grandeur. Whether you're an architecture enthusiast or simply appreciate the beauty of religious monuments, the Malaga Cathedral will not disappoint.

The cathedral stands proudly in the heart of Málaga's old town, a symbol of both faith and the city's cultural heritage. It took over two centuries to complete and reflects a blend of different architectural styles, including Gothic, Renaissance, and Baroque. Today, it continues to serve as a functional place of worship, hosting regular masses and special events, while also attracting thousands of visitors each year.

Why Visit the Malaga Cathedral?

🏰 **Stunning Architecture** – The cathedral blends Gothic, Renaissance, and Baroque elements, making it a masterpiece of Spanish architecture.

🖼 **Magnificent Interior** – Inside, you'll find awe-inspiring chapels, intricate wooden choir stalls, and stunning stained-glass windows that bring the cathedral to life.

📖 **Rich History** – Built between **1528** and **1782** on the site of a former mosque, the cathedral reflects Málaga's fascinating past, from Moorish rule to the Christian reconquest.

📷 **Panoramic Views** – Climb the cathedral's tower for an incredible 360-degree view of Málaga, stretching from the old town to the sparkling Mediterranean Sea.

🎵 **Cultural Events** – The cathedral hosts concerts, religious ceremonies, and special exhibitions throughout the year, offering visitors a unique way to experience its grandeur.

What to See Inside the Malaga Cathedral?

1. The Grand Interior

Stepping inside Málaga Cathedral is like entering an art museum. The **high vaulted ceilings**, massive stone pillars, and intricate carvings showcase the work of skilled artisans over several centuries. Highlights include:

- **The Choir Stalls** – Crafted by **Pedro de Mena**, the cathedral's wooden choir is one of the most spectacular in Spain, featuring over 40 beautifully carved figures of saints.

- **The Main Altar** – A striking mix of gold, marble, and religious paintings that captures the grandeur of Spanish religious art.

- **The Stained-Glass Windows** – Dating back to the 19th century, these vibrant windows fill the interior with colorful light.

- **The Chapels** – There are numerous chapels, each dedicated to different saints and showcasing impressive altarpieces and sculptures.

2. The Grand Facade & Entrance – As you approach the cathedral, you'll be greeted by its **towering exterior**, featuring intricate stonework and elegant sculptures. The main entrance, known as the **Door of the Chains (Puerta de las Cadenas)**, leads into a world of breathtaking architecture and religious history.

3. The Rooftop & Bell Tower – For one of the best **panoramic views in Málaga**, climb to the **cathedral's rooftop**. The **200-step staircase** takes you to a stunning viewpoint, where you can enjoy sweeping sights of the city, port, and coastline.

4. The Unfinished South Tower – One of the most famous features of Málaga Cathedral is its **missing second tower**, which led to its nickname, *La Manquita*. Construction was halted in the 18th century due to funding shortages, but rather than being a flaw, this detail has become one of the cathedral's most distinctive characteristics.

5. The Cathedral Museum – Located inside the cathedral, the **museum** houses religious artifacts, historical documents, and artwork that tells the story of Málaga Cathedral's long history. It's a great place to learn more about the city's religious and artistic heritage.

Ticket Prices & Opening Hours

🎟 **General Admission:** €8.
🎟 **Reduced Price:** €6 (students, seniors, and groups).
🎟 **Free Entry:** Sundays, 8:30 AM - 9:00 AM.

⏰ **Opening Hours:**

- **Monday to Saturday:** 10:00 AM - 6:00 PM.
- **Sundays:** 2:00 PM - 6:00 PM.

📍 **Address:** C. Molina Lario, 9, Distrito Centro, 29015 Málaga, Spain.

📞 **Phone:** +34 617 50 05 82.

✉ **Email:** info@museopicassomalaga.org

🌐 **Website:** https://malagacatedral.com/

How to Get There

🚶 **Walking:** Located in Málaga's historic center, the cathedral is just a short walk from major attractions like the **Alcazaba**, **Roman Theatre**, and **Picasso Museum**.

🚌 **Public Transport:** Take bus lines 1, 3, 4, or 11 to **Alameda Principal**, a short walk from the cathedral. The nearest metro station is **El Perchel** (15-minute walk).

🚗 **By Car:** There's limited parking in the old town, but nearby **public parking garages** are available at Plaza de la Marina and Calle Camas.

Where to Eat Nearby

After visiting Málaga Cathedral, take a break and enjoy some delicious Andalusian cuisine at any of these nearby restaurants:

🍽 **La Deriva** – A modern restaurant with a **fusion of Mediterranean and Andalusian flavors**, offering fresh seafood and gourmet dishes.

- **Address:** Alameda de Colón, 7, 29001 Málaga, Spain.

- **Phone:** +34 638 08 65 29.
- **Website:** https://laderiva.es/
- **Price Range:** Approximately **€20 to €40** per person.

🍽 **El Cortijo de Pepe** – A traditional Andalusian restaurant serving a variety of local dishes, including paella and grilled meats.

- **Address:** Plaza de la Merced, 2, Distrito Centro, 29012 Málaga, Spain.
- **Phone:** +34 952 22 40 71.
- **Website:** https://www.cortijodepepe.es/
- **Price Range:** Approximately **€20 to €40** per person.

Málaga Cathedral is more than just a place of worship—it's a **living monument to the city's history, art, and culture**. Whether you admire its grand architecture, explore its stunning interiors, or simply take in the breathtaking city views from the rooftop, this cathedral is a must-visit destination. If you're in Málaga, make sure to **step inside this iconic landmark and experience the beauty of its past and present**. From its fascinating history to its awe-inspiring design, Málaga Cathedral is truly a gem of Andalusia.

The Roman Theatre: Discovering Malaga's Ancient Past

The Roman Theatre: Discovering Málaga's Ancient Past

If you're a history lover or just curious about the past, the **Roman Theatre** in Málaga should definitely be on your list of places to explore. Nestled at the foot of the **Alcazaba fortress**, this ancient site takes you back to the time when **Málaga was part of the Roman Empire**. It's a perfect spot for anyone who wants to step into the past and imagine what life was like thousands of years ago.

The **Roman Theatre** is one of Málaga's **most significant historical landmarks**, and visiting it feels like uncovering a hidden treasure in the heart of the city. Even though the site has been around for centuries, it still holds a special place in the city's modern life. It's not just a relic from the past but a **living piece of history** that continues to shape the culture of Málaga today.

Why Visit the Roman Theatre?

🎭 **A Glimpse into Ancient Roman Life** – The Roman Theatre in Málaga is one of the best-preserved theatres from Roman times, and it gives you a unique chance to imagine what performances, rituals, and daily life might have looked like.

⌛ **The History** – Built in the 1st century BC, this theatre was used for **dramas, comedies, and performances** in ancient times. It's incredible to think about the **history** that happened in this spot over 2000 years ago.

🏛 **The Location** – Right next to the **Alcazaba,** this theatre is a **stone's throw away from Málaga's most famous attractions**, so it's easy to combine your visit with a stroll through the city.

📷 **Great Photo Opportunities** – With its impressive **columns, stone seating, and grand stage**, this site is a photographer's dream. Whether you're a professional or just snapping a quick pic with your phone, the theatre offers stunning views for every angle.

What You'll Find at the Roman Theatre

1. The Theatre's Structure

The Roman Theatre follows the **classic design** of Roman amphitheaters, with a **semi-circular cavea** (seating area), an **orchestra** where performers once stood, and a **scaena** (stage). Despite centuries of wear and modifications, much of its original structure remains intact, offering an authentic look at Roman engineering. The impressive stone walls have withstood the test of time, and the theatre is still used for performances during special events, making it a living link to the past.

2. The Archaeological Museum

One of the best parts of visiting the Roman Theatre is the **nearby museum (**Museo del Teatro Romano de Cartagena), a museum that showcases some of the **artifacts** found in the area. Inside, you'll see **Roman sculptures**, **pottery**, and **inscriptions**, which tell the story of the theatre's history and its role in the community.

3. A Walk-Through History

As you explore, you'll walk past **original stone seating**, remains of the **stage area**, and even sections of the **original entrance gates**. Standing in this space, it's easy to imagine the excitement of Roman citizens as they gathered for performances centuries ago.

Opening Hours & Ticket Prices

🎟 **General Admission**: Free entry.

⏰ **Opening Hours**:

- **Tuesday to Saturday**: 10:00 AM – 6:00 PM.

- **Monday**: Closed.

- **Sunday**: 10:00 AM – 4:00 PM.

Visitor Information:

📍 **Address**: Calle Alcazabilla, 29015 Málaga, Spain.

📞 **Phone**: +34 951 926 290.

✉️ **Email**: teatroromanomalaga@malaga.eu

🌐 **Website**: https://www.juntadeandalucia.es/

How to Get There

🚶 **Walking**: The Roman Theatre is located right in the heart of Málaga, so it's a short walk from many other city landmarks, including the **Alcazaba** and **Málaga Cathedral**. If you're already exploring the old town, you'll find it's just a few minutes away.

🚌 **Public Transport**: You can take bus **35** or **40** to the **Alcazaba** stop, which is a short walk from the Roman Theatre. Alternatively, take the **metro** to the **El Perchel station**, which is about a 15-minute walk to the site.

🚗 **By Car**: Parking in the historic center is limited, but nearby garages like **Parking Alcazaba** offer convenient options.

Where to Eat Nearby

After exploring the Roman Theatre, you'll likely be ready to enjoy a bite to eat. Málaga's historic center has some great options just a stone's throw away:

🍴 **El Soldadito de Plomo** – A lively café located in Cartagena, Murcia, offering a cozy atmosphere and a variety of homemade desserts and beverages. It's an ideal spot for those seeking a relaxed dining experience.

- **Address**: Calle Príncipe de Vergara, 1, 30202 Cartagena, Murcia, Spain.
- **Phone**: +34 868 96 68 12.
- **Price Range**: Approximately €5 to €14 per person.

🍴 **La Taberna del Pintxo** – A local favorite serving **authentic Spanish pintxos**, fresh seafood, and Iberian ham

- **Address**: Calle Alarcón Luján 12, Esq, C. Antonio Baena Gómez, nº 3, 29005 Málaga, Spain.
- **Phone**: +34 638 78 31 59.
- **Website**: https://www.latabernadelpintxo-malaga.com/

The **Roman Theatre of Málaga** is more than just an ancient monument—it's a **testament to the city's dynamic past**. Exploring this site allows you to experience **Roman Málaga**, understand how **entertainment shaped society**, and appreciate the **architectural brilliance** of the ancient world.

Whether you're a **history enthusiast**, an **architecture lover**, or simply someone who enjoys a good cultural experience, this theatre is **a must-see attraction** in Málaga. Make sure to add it to your itinerary and **step back in time** as you uncover the fascinating stories hidden within its stones.

94 | MALAGA TRAVEL GUIDE 2025

Chapter 4

Outdoor Adventures and Natural Escapes in Malaga

Málaga is not just a city of history and culture—it's also a gateway to incredible outdoor experiences and natural wonders. From the pristine beaches that line the Costa del Sol to the lush hiking trails of Montes de Málaga, the region offers a perfect mix of adventure and tranquility. Whether you prefer water sports, scenic walks, or day trips to nearby coastal gems, this chapter will guide you through the best outdoor activities Málaga has to offer.

Malaga's Beaches: Playa de la Malagueta and Beyond

Málaga's coastline is one of the city's greatest treasures, offering a blend of sunny relaxation and lively atmosphere. Whether you're a sun seeker, a watersport enthusiast, or just looking for a peaceful place to unwind, Málaga's beaches have something for everyone. From the bustling **Playa de la Malagueta** to the quieter, hidden gems, the beaches here offer a taste of the Mediterranean lifestyle.

Playa de la Malagueta: The Heart of Málaga's Beach Scene

Playa de la Malagueta is the city's most famous beach and is where both locals and tourists flock for sunbathing, swimming, and a vibrant seaside atmosphere. Located just a short walk from the city center, it's easy to reach and hard to miss. The beach is framed by a promenade lined with **palm trees** and dotted with restaurants and beach bars offering **refreshing drinks**, **tapas**, and the freshest seafood.

Why Visit Playa de la Malagueta?

🏖 **Perfect for Sunbathing** – The beach has golden sand and plenty of space to spread out your towel and soak up the Mediterranean sun. It's not too crowded, so you can find your perfect spot to relax.

🌊 **Ideal for Swimming** – The waters are generally calm, making it a great place for a dip. Whether you're swimming or just wading in the shallow areas, the clear waters are inviting.

🍹 **Beach Bars & Restaurants** – Playa de la Malagueta is home to numerous beach bars known as **chiringuitos**, where you can grab a refreshing drink or enjoy a meal right by the sea. From **fried fish** to **grilled sardines**, there's a wide variety of local dishes to savor.

Things to Do Nearby:

Take a walk along the **Muelle 1 Pier** – Just a short distance from the beach, Muelle 1 offers shopping, restaurants, and beautiful views of the marina.

Rent a bike or take a stroll along the **Paseo Marítimo** – The promenade stretches along the coast and is perfect for a leisurely walk or bike ride.

Beyond Playa de la Malagueta: Hidden Beach Gems in Málaga

While Playa de la Malagueta is the most well-known, there are plenty of other beaches in Málaga that offer a more **peaceful vibe** and **stunning natural beauty**. Let's take a look at a few of the best ones:

Playa del Palo: A Taste of Local Life

If you're looking for a more authentic, local beach experience, **Playa del Palo** is the perfect spot. Located in the eastern part of Málaga, this beach offers a quieter atmosphere compared to the more touristy areas. Here, you'll find locals enjoying their day at the beach, and the **chiringuitos** serve some of the best **seafood** in the city.

The area is more residential, so it's perfect if you're looking for a more relaxed and genuine **Málaga beach vibe**. You can enjoy the calm waters, take in the scenic views, and enjoy the delicious food from the local beach bars.

Playa de la Misericordia: A Hidden Gem

Playa de la Misericordia is a less crowded beach that's great for those seeking a peaceful retreat. It's located slightly further from the city center, making it less frequented by tourists. This beach is known for its **wide expanse of sand** and **clear waters**, perfect for relaxing or going for a leisurely swim.

There's also a **long promenade** where you can walk, run, or enjoy the fresh sea breeze. If you're in the mood for a quieter beach experience, Playa de la Misericordia is one of the best options in Málaga.

Playa de Guadalmar: Secluded & Scenic

Playa de Guadalmar is a bit of a hidden treasure, located on the outskirts of the city, and is not as well-known as the other beaches. This beach offers a **more natural setting** with fewer people, making it ideal for those who want a break from the crowds. The beach is surrounded by dunes, and the area is quite peaceful, perfect for a day of **relaxation** and **solitude**.

It's also great for **family outings**, as the waters are calm and the beach is safe for children. If you want to enjoy the **natural beauty** of Málaga's coastline without the hustle and bustle, this beach is worth visiting.

How to Get to Málaga's Beaches

Getting to any of these beaches is pretty easy, thanks to Málaga's excellent public transport system. Most beaches, like **Playa de la Malagueta**, are just a short walk or bus ride from the city center. For the quieter spots, such as **Playa de Guadalmar**, you may need to take a short **bus ride** or **taxi**.

🚶 **Walking**: Most of the city's beaches are within walking distance from the historic center, especially Playa de la Malagueta, which is just a 10-15-minute walk from the city center.

🚌 **Public Transport**: Bus routes **11, 35, and 40** connect the city center with the beaches. For **Playa de Guadalmar**, the **bus line 13** will get you there.

🚗 **By Car**: If you have a car, parking is available near the beaches, although during peak summer months, it can be difficult to find a spot at the more popular beaches. It's often better to park a little further away and walk to the beach.

Things to Do at Málaga's Beaches

- **Watersports**: Many of the beaches, especially Playa de la Malagueta, offer **kayaks**, **paddle boards**, and **jet skis** for rent. If you're feeling adventurous, this is a fun way to spend the day.

- **Beach Volleyball**: Playa de la Malagueta is home to several beach volleyball courts, so if you're up for a friendly match, bring a ball and join in!
- **Relaxing**: If you just want to relax, lay back in the sand, read a book, or enjoy the warm weather. Málaga's beaches provide the perfect setting for unwinding.

Nearby Dining: Savoring Local Flavors by the Sea

After a day at the beach, you'll want to grab a bite to eat. Fortunately, Málaga's beaches are lined with **chiringuitos**, where you can sample traditional Spanish seafood dishes and enjoy a cold drink. Here are a couple of top spots:

🍽 **El Tintero** (Playa del Palo)

Known for its **fried fish** and **seafood platters**, this popular restaurant serves up the freshest catches of the day in a casual, laid-back setting. The **waiters** even bring the food to your table on trays, and you can choose what you want directly from them.

- **Address**: Av. Salvador Allende, 340, Málaga-Este, 29017 Málaga.

- **Phone:** +34 650 68 09 56.
- **Website:** https://eltinteromalaga.com/
- **Price Range:** Approximately €20 to €30 per person.

🍴 Chiringuito El Cabra (Playa de la Misericordia)

For an authentic **beachside dining experience**, head to **El Cabra**. It's a great spot to enjoy a meal while looking out over the ocean. The specialty here is **grilled sardines** and other **local seafood dishes**.

- **Address:** Paseo Marítimo el Pedregal, 17, Málaga-Este, 29017 Málaga.
- **Phone:** +34 680 54 41 26.
- **Website:** https://restauranteelcabra.es/
- **Price Range:** Approximately €20 to €30 per person.

Whether you're in the mood for a lively beach day or a peaceful escape, Málaga's coastline has it all. From the iconic **Playa de la Malagueta** to the hidden gems like **Playa de Guadalmar**, you'll find the perfect beach to suit your needs.

Day Trips to Nearby Beaches: Nerja, Torremolinos, and Marbella

---

While Málaga has some stunning beaches right on its doorstep, the surrounding coastal towns also boast beautiful shores and unique vibes. If you're looking to explore beyond the city, here are three fantastic beach destinations that are perfect for a day trip. Whether you're after crystal-clear waters, quaint seaside towns, or a lively atmosphere, these spots will leave you with unforgettable memories.

Nerja: A Picturesque Escape on the Costa del Sol

Located about **50 kilometers** east of Málaga, **Nerja** is a charming town that offers more than just beautiful beaches. Known for its rugged coastline, pristine beaches, and a historic town center, Nerja is an excellent destination for anyone looking to experience a bit of everything.

Why Visit Nerja?

📧 **Beaches** – The beaches in Nerja are some of the most beautiful on the Costa del Sol. **Playa Burriana** is the most popular, with clear waters, soft sand, and plenty of beach bars (known as **chiringuitos**) to enjoy a refreshing drink. If you prefer something quieter, head to **Playa de Maro**, a more secluded beach surrounded by cliffs.

Old Town Charm – Nerja's **old town** is a picturesque maze of narrow streets, whitewashed buildings, and quaint squares. Take a leisurely walk through this lovely area, and don't miss a visit to the **Balcon de Europa**.

Hiking and Nature Trails: Montes de Málaga Natural Park

If you're a nature enthusiast or simply want to escape the hustle and bustle of the city, the **Montes de Málaga Natural Park** is the perfect place for you. Just a short drive from Málaga's city center, this expansive park offers a peaceful retreat with plenty of hiking trails, wildlife, and stunning views of the surrounding mountains and Mediterranean coastline. Whether you're looking for a challenging hike or a casual stroll through nature, the Montes de Málaga has something for everyone.

Why Visit Montes de Málaga Natural Park?

🌳 **Natural Beauty** – This park is a treasure trove of natural beauty. The lush forests of **pine trees**, **oak groves**, and **wild olive trees** create a serene atmosphere that feels far removed from the city. Along the trails, you'll come across **streams**, **waterfalls**, and **breathtaking viewpoints** where you can pause and take in the scenery.

🚶 **Hiking Trails for All Levels** – Whether you're an experienced hiker or just want a peaceful walk in nature, the Montes de Málaga offers a variety of trails for all fitness levels. One of the most popular routes is the **"Ruta de los Cazadores"**

(Hunters' Trail), which is a relatively easy **4.5-kilometer** circular path that provides panoramic views of the **Malaga Valley** and the Mediterranean. If you're looking for something more challenging, try the **"Sierra de las Tres Villas"**, a more difficult trail that leads to the top of the **Cerro de la Morilla**, offering stunning views of the surrounding mountains and Málaga.

🦉 **Wildlife Spotting** – This park is also home to a variety of wildlife. Look out for **wild boar, foxes,** and **mountain goats**, as well as an array of bird species like **eagles** and **buzzards**. If you're into birdwatching, be sure to bring a pair of binoculars!

🌿 **Picnic Areas and Rest Stops** – After a hike, enjoy a relaxing break at one of the park's designated **picnic areas**. These spots are perfect for taking in the surroundings and enjoying a meal outdoors while soaking up the tranquility of the natural world.

How to Get to Montes de Málaga Natural Park:

- **By Car**: The easiest way to reach Montes de Málaga is by car. The **A-7000** road leads directly into the park from Málaga, taking approximately **20 minutes** from the city center. Parking is available at various trailheads and picnic areas.

- **Public Transport:** Currently, **no direct public transport** serves the park, but you can take a bus to **Ciudad Jardín** and then take a short taxi ride to the park entrance.
- **By Bike**: Cycling enthusiasts can ride from Málaga to the park via the **A-7000**, though be prepared for steep climbs.

Things to Keep in Mind:

- **What to Bring**: Make sure you wear comfortable shoes, bring plenty of water, and pack some snacks for your hike. Sunscreen is also a good idea, especially if you're going on a sunny day.
- **Weather**: The park is open year-round, but it's best to visit in the spring or fall when the temperatures are milder. Summer can get quite hot, so morning hikes are recommended to avoid the heat.
- **Guided Tours**: If you prefer a guided hike, there are local companies that offer organized walking tours of the park, where you'll get to learn more about the area's history, flora, and fauna from an expert guide.

Opening Hours & Ticket Prices

🎟 **General Admission**: Free entry.

⏰ Opening Hours:

Open 24/7, though it's best to visit during daylight hours.

Contact Information:

- **Address**: Montes de Málaga Natural Park, 29190 Málaga, Spain.

- **Email**: info@malagaturismo.com

- **Website**: https://visita.malaga.eu/

Montes de Málaga Natural Park is more than just a green space—it's a **sanctuary of biodiversity, adventure, and cultural heritage**. Whether you're seeking a peaceful nature walk, a thrilling hike, or a chance to explore Andalusia's rich ecological landscape, this park has something for everyone. So, next time you're in Málaga, take a break from the city's dynamic streets and **immerse yourself in the natural beauty** of this breathtaking park!

Water Sports: Surfing, Paddleboarding, and More

Malaga isn't just about beautiful beaches—it's a haven for water sports lovers. Whether you're an adrenaline junkie or just looking to try something new, there's a wide range of activities you can enjoy on the Mediterranean. From **surfing** the waves to paddling out in a **stand-up paddleboard (SUP)**, there's something for every type of water enthusiast. In this chapter, we will share some of the best places to dive into these exciting activities!

Surfing in Malaga

Though it might not be the first destination that comes to mind for surfing, Malaga offers some great spots to catch the waves. The **Costa del Sol** is known for its sunny weather and mild Mediterranean waves, making it perfect for both beginners and intermediate surfers. There are several surf schools and rental spots scattered along the coast, so you won't have to go far to find a good wave.

Top Surfing Spots:

1. **Playa de la Misericordia** – Just a short drive from the city center, this beach is great for surfers of all levels. It's popular

among locals and offers plenty of space for everyone to catch a wave. During the summer, it's a bit more crowded, but you'll still find good waves.

2. **El Palo Beach** – Known for its laid-back vibe, **El Palo** is a fantastic spot for both surfing and soaking in the local atmosphere. Here, you'll find more consistent waves, and it's less touristy, which means you'll have a more relaxed experience.

Where to Rent Surf Gear:

Kayak & Bike

A versatile rental service offering a range of water sports equipment, including surfboards and paddleboards.

- **Address:** C. Quitapenas, 7, Málaga-Este, 29017 Málaga, Spain.
- **Website:** https://kayakybike.es/en/home/
- **Phone:** +34 662 05 07 13.
- **Price Range**: Surfboard rentals start at €10 per hour.
- **Opening Hours**: Daily, 10:30 AM - 7:30 PM.

Paddleboarding in Malaga

For something a little more relaxed but equally fun, **paddleboarding** is one of the most popular water activities in

Malaga. It's a fantastic way to explore the coastline at your own pace while getting a great full-body workout. Whether you're paddling along the calm waters of the bay or exploring hidden coves, you'll have an unforgettable time.

Best Paddleboarding Locations:

1. **La Malagueta Beach** – Located near the city center, **La Malagueta** is one of the best places to paddleboard in Malaga. The waters are usually calm, and you can easily rent a board from one of the local kiosks on the beach. Plus, you get great views of the **Alcazaba Fortress** and the **Mediterranean**.

2. **Playa de la Caleta** – For a more peaceful experience, **Playa de la Caleta** offers calm waters and fewer crowds. It's the perfect spot for beginners or those looking for a tranquil paddleboarding experience away from the bustling beach.

Where to Rent Paddleboards:

Flex-Watersports

Offering flexible rental periods, **Flex-Watersports** provides paddleboards at €35 per day, €60 for a weekend, and €150 per week. They also offer delivery services within Málaga.

- **Address:** Calle Reding 10, Edificio Santa Monica, 29016 Málaga, Spain.

- **Website:** https://flex-watersports.com/malaga/
- **Opening Hours**: Daily, 8:00 AM - 8:00PM.

Other Water Sports in Malaga

If you're looking for more excitement on the water, **Malaga** also has plenty of options to try something different. From jet skiing to kayaking, there's no shortage of ways to get your adrenaline pumping.

- **Jet Skiing** – For those seeking a thrill, **jet skiing** is a fun way to explore the coast. Most of the beaches offer rentals, with many of them providing guided tours along the stunning coastline.

- **Kayaking** – If you prefer something more low-key, **kayaking** is another fantastic way to experience the waters of Malaga. Paddle along the calm coves, explore hidden beaches, or even head out to the nearby **Gibralfaro Castle** for a unique view of the city.

Where to Book Water Sports Activities:

Jet Ski Costa del Sol

- **Address:** Puerto Deportivo Fuengirola, 29640 Fuengirola, Málaga.
- **Website:** https://jetskicostadelsol.com/
- **Phone:** +34 611 20 81 16.
- **Price Range:** Approximately €50 to €120 per person, depending on rental duration.
- **Opening Hours:** Daily, 10:30 AM - 8:30 PM.

Jet Ski Costa del Sol Malaga Water Sports is a go-to rental service for **high-speed jet ski rides**, offering guided tours and solo rentals for a thrilling experience on the water.

Tips for Water Sports in Malaga:

- **Safety First:** Always wear a life jacket, especially if you're new to water sports. Most rental shops provide them, but it's important to ensure you're wearing one for your safety.

- **Sun Protection:** Don't forget the sunscreen! Malaga can get quite hot, and you'll be out in the sun for hours.

- **Hydrate:** It's easy to forget to drink water while you're having fun, but make sure to stay hydrated, especially after physical activities like surfing or paddleboarding.

- **Check the Weather**: Water conditions can change quickly, so always check the forecast before heading out, especially if you're planning to surf or kayak in open waters.

Whether you're trying your hand at **surfing**, enjoying a **paddleboarding** session, or seeking an adrenaline rush with **jet skiing**, Malaga's coast offers some incredible opportunities to enjoy the water. With the stunning beaches, the warm Mediterranean climate, and plenty of equipment rental options, it's no wonder that water sports are so popular here.

Chapter 5

A Culinary Journey Through Malaga

Málaga's culinary scene is a true reflection of its rich cultural heritage, Mediterranean coastline, and passion for fresh, flavorful food. From the lively tapas bars in the city center to the refined elegance of Michelin-starred restaurants, Málaga offers something for every palate. This chapter explores the city's most iconic dishes, the dynamic tapas culture, local wines, and the best spots to savor seafood or street food. Whether you're a foodie or simply curious about Málaga's gastronomic delights, this chapter will guide you through the flavors that make this city a culinary destination.

Tapas Culture: Must-Try Dishes and Local Favorites

When in **Malaga**, you simply can't miss out on the world-renowned **tapas** culture. These small, flavorful dishes are an integral part of Spanish cuisine and offer the perfect way to sample a variety of tastes without committing to one large meal. It's a tradition that brings people together, encourages conversation, and—most importantly—celebrates great food.

In this section, we're diving into the must-try **tapas** dishes that you'll find all around **Malaga**. Whether you're a seasoned foodie or just starting to explore the flavors of Spain, these local favorites are sure to hit the spot.

1. Espetos (Grilled Sardines)

One of the most iconic dishes of **Malaga**, **espetos** are fresh sardines skewered and grilled over open flames. This dish is a true reflection of the **Mediterranean** way of life. Best enjoyed at the beachside with a cold beer in hand, **espetos** are a must-try when in **Malaga**.

Where to Try Espetos:

Chiringuito La Farola

- o **Address**: Paseo Marítimo Pablo Ruiz Picasso, 54, 29016 Málaga, Spain.

- o **Website**: https://www.chiringuitolafarola.com/

- o **Phone**: +34 673 12 44 66.

- o **Price Range:** Approximately €10 - €20 per person.

This beachfront gem is known for its **authentic espetos**, grilled to perfection over a **wood-burning fire pit**. The combination of **fresh sea air, ocean views, and expertly prepared sardines** makes it a go-to spot for locals and visitors alike. Pair your espetos with a **cold beer or a glass of local white wine** for the perfect seaside meal.

2. Patatas Bravas

You'll find **patatas bravas** all across Spain, but **Malaga** has its own twist on this popular dish. Fried potatoes are served with a spicy tomato sauce or aioli, offering the perfect balance of crispy and creamy flavors. The sauce can vary from mild to quite spicy, depending on where you go, so be prepared to experience different variations.

Where to Try Patatas Bravas:

Las Merchanas

- o **Address**: Calle Mosquera, 5, 29008 Málaga, Spain.

- o **Price Range**: Approximately €4 - €10 per person.

A hidden gem in Málaga, **Las Merchanas** serves **Patatas Bravas with a unique Andalusian twist**. Their sauce is a **perfect balance of smoky, tangy, and spicy flavors**, making it a local favorite. The rustic decor and traditional vibe add to the charm of this lively tapas bar.

3. Jamón Ibérico

No trip to **Malaga** is complete without trying **Jamón Ibérico**, Spain's famous cured ham. The rich, melt-in-your-mouth flavor of **Jamón Ibérico** is something that will leave a lasting impression. Whether served in thin slices or wrapped around **manchego cheese**, it's a tapas' favorite you can't miss.

Where to Try Jamón Ibérico:

Los Patios de Beatas

- **Address**: Calle Beatas, 43, 29008 Málaga, Spain.

- **Website**: www.lospatiosdebeatas.com

- **Phone**: +34 952 21 03 50.

- **Price Range**: Approximately €15 - €40 per person.

For a **refined take on Jamón Ibérico**, **Los Patios de Beatas** offers expertly **sliced cured ham**, paired with a **curated selection of wines** from their impressive cellar. The **tapas-style servings** allow guests to sample different varieties of **high-quality Ibérico ham**, all in an elegant **wine bar setting** that blends history with modern sophistication.

4. Croquetas (Croquettes)

Another Spanish classic, **croquetas** are deep-fried balls of creamy goodness filled with a variety of fillings like **ham**, **cheese**, or **spinach**. They're crispy on the outside and soft on the inside, making them the ultimate comfort food.

Where to Try Croquetas:

El Pimpi

- **Address**: Calle Granada, 62, 29015 Málaga, Spain.

- **Website**: https://www.elpimpi.com/

- **Phone**: +34 952 22 54 03.

- **Price Range**: Approximately €6 - €18 per person.

This **iconic Málaga bodega** is famous for its **homemade croquetas**, especially the **jamón ibérico (Iberian ham) and seafood varieties**. Pair them with a glass of Málaga's **sweet wine** and enjoy the **historic charm** of one of the city's most beloved restaurants.

5. Ensalada Malagueña (Malaga-Style Salad)

The **Ensalada Malagueña** is a refreshing salad made with **cod**, **potatoes**, **onions**, and **oranges**. This light yet flavorful dish is perfect for a warm afternoon, especially when paired with a chilled glass of **Spanish white wine**.

Where to Try Ensalada Malagueña:

Casa Lola

- **Address**: Calle Granada, 46, 29015 Málaga, Spain

- **Website**: https://menu.tipsipro.com

- **Phone**: +34 952 22 38 14.

- **Price Range**: Approximately €7 to €20 per person.

A favorite among locals and visitors alike, **Casa Lola** serves a **classic yet modern take on Ensalada Malagueña**. The balance of **salted cod, juicy oranges, and high-quality olive oil** makes this dish a refreshing choice. Enjoy it in the **vibrant and lively setting** of this popular tapas bar.

6. Gambas al Pil-Pil (Garlic Shrimp)

Gambas al Pil-Pil is a mouthwatering tapas dish made with shrimp, **garlic**, **chili**, and **olive oil**. It's simple yet packed with flavor. The shrimp is sautéed in sizzling oil with garlic and a bit of spice, creating a dish that's perfectly balanced and addictive.

Where to Try Gambas al Pil-Pil:

El Tapeo de Cervantes

- **Address**: Calle Cárcer, 8, 29012 Málaga, Spain.

- **Email**: https://eltapeodecervantes.com/

- **Phone**: +34 952 60 94 58.

- **Price Range**: Approximately €8 - €20 per person.

A charming, **intimate tapas bar** located in the heart of Málaga, **El Tapeo de Cervantes** is renowned for its **authentic Andalusian flavors**. Their **Gambas al Pil-Pil** is a standout dish, cooked in **rich extra virgin olive oil with just the right touch of spice**. Pair it with a glass of local **white wine or fino sherry** for the perfect culinary experience.

Tips for Enjoying Tapas in Malaga:

- **Order a variety**: Don't be afraid to order multiple dishes and share with friends. Tapas are meant to be enjoyed in good company, so try a little bit of everything!

- **Take your time**: Tapas are meant to be savored slowly, with great conversation. Don't rush—enjoy the experience.

- **Pair with local drinks**: Be sure to pair your tapas with a local wine or **sherry**. In **Malaga**, you'll find a variety of **sweet wines** that pair perfectly with your meal.

Tapas are more than just food—they're a way to experience the heart of **Malaga's** culinary culture. So, whether you're sitting at a beachside restaurant or tucked away in a quaint little tapas bar, take your time to savor the flavors, and don't forget to enjoy the company you're with.

Fine Dining and Michelin-Star Restaurants

When you think of **Malaga**, you might imagine the beach, tapas, and vibrant street life. But did you know that this coastal city also has a growing reputation in the world of **fine dining**? Whether you're looking to celebrate a special occasion or simply want to indulge in a memorable meal, **Malaga** offers several Michelin-starred restaurants that will elevate your dining experience to a whole new level.

In this chapter, we'll explore some of **Malaga's** finest dining options, from Michelin-star restaurants to innovative fine dining spots. Get ready for an unforgettable culinary journey!

1. Restaurante José Carlos García – A Michelin Star Experience

Restaurante José Carlos García is one of the top Michelin-star restaurants in **Malaga**, offering an exquisite dining experience with a focus on local, seasonal ingredients. **Chef José Carlos García** brings a unique twist to traditional Spanish cuisine, blending modern techniques with Andalusian flavors. The restaurant's creative and elegant presentation will impress even the most discerning food lovers.

What to Expect:

- A tasting menu that changes with the seasons.
- Dishes like **"Mojama" (cured tuna)** or **"Foie gras with truffle**" that combine local flavors with refined technique.
- A sleek, modern interior with breathtaking views of the **Malaga port**.

Where to Find José Carlos García:

- **Address**: Muelle Uno, Puerto de Málaga, 29001 Málaga, Spain.
- **Website**: www.restaurantejcg.com
- **Phone**: +34 952 00 35 88.
- **Price Range:** Approximately 100+ per person.

Located in the **Muelle 1** area, this restaurant offers the perfect blend of spectacular food and stunning views of the harbor. Be sure to book ahead, as this Michelin-starred restaurant is a popular choice among locals and tourists alike.

2. Restaurante Skina – A Journey Through Andalusian Cuisine

For those seeking a more intimate and personalized experience, **Restaurante Skina** offers an exceptional tasting menu that showcases the best of **Andalusian** cuisine. With two Michelin stars, **Skina** is known for its innovative approach to traditional Spanish dishes. The restaurant's intimate setting, with just a few tables, ensures a more private and exclusive dining experience.

What to Expect:

- Innovative dishes with fresh, local ingredients.
- A focus on creating a balance between traditional flavors and modern cooking techniques.
- Personalized wine pairings from their curated collection of Spanish wines.

Where to Find Restaurante Skina:

- **Address**: Avenue Cánovas del Castillo, 9, 29603 Marbella, Málaga, Spain.
- **Email**: https://www.restauranteskina.com/
- **Phone**: +34 604 48 63 03.
- **Price Range:** Approximately 100+ per person.

Located in the **historic center of Malaga**, **Skina** is a must-visit for those who truly want to experience the art of fine dining. The cozy atmosphere makes it perfect for an intimate, high-end meal.

3. Messina – A Michelin Star with Mediterranean Flair

If you're in the mood for Mediterranean-inspired cuisine, **Messina** is the place to be. With one Michelin star, **Chef Mauricio Giovanini** creates stunning, creative dishes that highlight the fresh seafood and vegetables found along the Mediterranean coast. **Messina**'s focus is on innovative cooking, but it always stays true to the roots of the Mediterranean diet.

What to Expect:

- A tasting menu that features Mediterranean flavors, with an emphasis on seafood.
- Dishes like **sea urchin** with **seaweed** and **lobster** with **caviar**.
- Beautiful plating that makes each dish feel like a work of art.

Where to Find Messina:

- **Address**: Avenida Severo Ochoa, 12, 29603 Marbella, Málaga.
- **Website**: www.restaurantemessina.com
- **Phone**: +34 952 86 48 95.
- **Price Range:** Approximately 100+ per person.

Messina is tucked away in the **El Limonar** district, just a short walk from the **city center**. With its elegant ambiance and top-notch food, this is a place to relax, savor, and enjoy every bite.

4. El Lago – A Michelin Star in the Heart of Nature

If you're looking for a Michelin-star restaurant that also offers stunning views of nature, **El Lago** is the perfect spot. Nestled in the heart of the **Greenway of Marbella**, this restaurant combines gourmet cuisine with a relaxing atmosphere. Known for its focus on local and organic ingredients, **El Lago** serves dishes that highlight the flavors of the surrounding mountains and coast.

What to Expect:

- Creative Mediterranean cuisine with a focus on seasonal, local products.
- A beautiful, peaceful setting overlooking a lake, which adds a sense of tranquility to your dining experience.
- Dishes like **wild sea bass with black garlic** or **local lamb with rosemary**.

Where to Find El Lago:

- **Address**: Avenida de Las Cumbres, s/n, 29604 Marbella, Málaga, Spain

- **Website**: www.restauranteellago.com
- **Phone**: +34 952 83 23 71.
- **Price Range:** Approximately 100+ per person.

Located just outside **Marbella**, **El Lago** is ideal for those who want to combine fine dining with the beauty of nature. The peaceful surroundings will allow you to fully immerse yourself in the exceptional flavors of the region.

Tips for Fine Dining in Malaga:

- **Dress Code**: Many of these Michelin-star restaurants have a smart-casual or formal dress code, so be sure to check before you go.
- **Reservations**: Be sure to make reservations ahead of time, especially if you plan to dine at one of the Michelin-starred spots. These places fill up quickly.
- **Wine Pairing**: Don't miss out on the wine pairing options. Spain has some of the best wines in the world, and the sommeliers at these restaurants are experts at selecting the perfect wine to complement your meal.

Whether you're in the mood for an intimate, gourmet meal at **Skina** or a chic, modern dining experience at **José Carlos García**, **Malaga** offers plenty of options for those looking to indulge. Treat yourself to the flavors of **Andalucia** with these

Michelin-star restaurants and create unforgettable memories through their exceptional food, service, and ambiance.

Malaga's Wine: Exploring Local Varieties

When you think of **Malaga**, your mind probably wanders to the vibrant culture, sunny beaches, and, of course, the **delicious food**. But what about the wine? **Malaga** has a rich **winemaking history**, with its **local varieties** offering a unique taste of the region's soil, sun, and traditions. Whether you're a wine connoisseur or someone who just enjoys a glass or two, this chapter will introduce you to **Malaga's wines** and where to explore them.

1. Malaga's Sweet Wine: The Star of the Region

The most famous wine from **Malaga** is undoubtedly its **sweet wine**, made from a variety of **Muscat** grapes. This wine has been a staple in the region for centuries, dating back to the ancient Greeks and Romans. The **sweet Malaga wine** is a treat for anyone with a sweet tooth, offering deep, fruity flavors balanced with a touch of **honey** and **caramel**.

What to Expect:

Malaga's sweet wine is rich and full-bodied, perfect for sipping after dinner or pairing with dessert.

The wine's **flavors** range from **citrus** to **dried fruit**, with a smooth, velvety finish.

If you want to experience the best **Malaga wine**, visiting a **local vineyard** is a must. Many of the vineyards that produce this famous sweet wine offer guided tours where you can learn about the winemaking process and taste different varieties of **Malaga wine**.

2. Bodegas Málaga Virgen – A Historic Vineyard with a Rich Legacy

Located in the heart of the **Malaga** wine region, **Bodegas Málaga Virgen** is one of the oldest and most prestigious wineries in the area. Established in the 19th century, this family-run vineyard is famous for its **Muscatel** wines and traditional winemaking methods.

What to Expect:

- A deep dive into **Malaga's winemaking history**, with a focus on **sweet wines**.
- Tasting tours that allow you to sample a variety of wines, from the **classic Malaga sweet wine** to **dry whites** and **reds**.
- The chance to walk through the **vineyards** and see where the magic happens.

Where to Find Bodegas Málaga Virgen:

- **Address**: A-92 km 132, Finca Vistahermosa, 29520 Fuente de Piedra, Málaga, Spain.
- **Website**: www.malagavirgen.com
- **Phone**: +34 952 31 94 54.
- **Price Range:** Wine tastings begin from approximately €10 to €35 per person.
- **Opening Hours:** Monday to Friday 7:30 AM - 3:30 PM. Closed on Saturdays and Sundays.

Visiting **Bodegas Málaga Virgen** will give you a hands-on experience of the wine production process, from **grape harvesting** to bottling. If you're looking to dive into the world of Malaga's wines, this place is a must-visit.

3. La Cueva de 1900 – A Wine Experience with a Twist

Looking to enjoy some of **Malaga's finest wines** while also learning about the history of the region? **La Cueva de 1900** offers a unique experience, where you can taste wines from **local vineyards** while also exploring a collection of **vintage wine bottles** and learning about the area's winemaking history. The wine cellar is set in a **beautiful underground space**, giving you an immersive experience that blends **history** with **flavor**.

What to Expect:

- A variety of **Malaga's sweet wines**, along with **vintage reds** and **white wines**.
- A guided tour of the **wine cellar**, where you'll learn about the region's history and winemaking techniques.
- The chance to taste wines paired with **local cheeses** and **charcuterie**.

Where to Find La Cueva de 1900:

- **Address**: Calle Martínez, 9, 29005 Málaga, Spain.
- **Website**: https://lacuevade1900.es/martinez-9/
- **Phone**: +34 952 22 39 76.
- **Price Range:** Approximately **€15 to €50** per person.
- **Opening Hours:** Sunday to Thursday 9:00 AM - 11:00 PM, Friday and Saturday 9:00 AM - 12:00 AM.

La Cueva de 1900 is perfect for wine lovers who want a more interactive experience that combines the best of **Malaga's wines** with a touch of **history**.

4. Vinoteca Los Patios de Beatas – A Modern Twist on Local Wine Tasting

For a more contemporary wine-tasting experience, **Vinoteca Málaga** is the place to go. Located near the city center, this modern wine bar offers a wide selection of **Malaga wines**, along **Find** with some international varieties. It's an excellent spot for those who want to explore the diverse range of wines that **Malaga** has to offer, from the **classic sweet wines** to more modern and dry reds.

What to Expect:

- A wide range of **local wines**, from well-known varieties to lesser-known gems.
- Tasting options that allow you to try multiple wines in small portions.
- A stylish, modern atmosphere that's perfect for enjoying wine with friends or as part of a special occasion.

Where to Vinoteca Los Patios de Beatas:

- **Address**: Calle Beatas, 43, 29008 Málaga, Spain.
- **Website**: https://lospatiosdebeatas.com/
- **Phone**: +34 952 21 03 50.
- **Price Range:** Approximately €20 to €50 per person
- **Opening Hours:** Daily, 1:00 PM - 5:00 PM, 8:00 PM - 12:00 AM.

Vinoteca Los Patios de Beatas is ideal for those looking to enjoy a wide variety of **local wines** in a relaxed yet modern setting.

Tips for Wine Lovers in Malaga:

- **Try Before You Buy**: Many local wineries offer tastings, so be sure to take advantage of this opportunity to sample before making a purchase.
- **Pairing Food with Wine**: For the full experience, try pairing your wine with local **cheeses** or **cured meats**. Malaga's **tapas culture** pairs beautifully with its wines.
- **Go on a Wine Tour**: If you want to explore **Malaga's vineyards** in more depth, consider booking a **wine tour**. This is a great way to experience the beauty of the region while learning about the winemaking process.

Whether you're sipping **Malaga's sweet wines** on a sunny terrace or diving into the world of **local vineyards**, there's no shortage of ways to explore the rich wine culture in this stunning city. Make sure to visit one of the **wineries** or **wine bars** we've recommended for a deeper understanding of the flavors and history that make **Malaga's wine** so special.

Street Food: Where to Eat Like a Local

When it comes to **Malaga**, there's no better way to experience the city's vibrant culture than by diving into its **street food scene**. Walking through the bustling streets, you'll find small vendors and **local markets** offering quick, affordable, and mouth-watering bites. Whether you're on the go or just looking to experience the city's flavors, this chapter is your guide to eating like a **local**.

1. Churros: The Sweet Breakfast Treat

Start your day like a true **Malagueño** with a **churro**. This deep-fried, doughy pastry is crispy on the outside, soft on the inside, and dusted with sugar. If you're craving something sweet and satisfying, churros with **hot chocolate** is the go-to breakfast for many locals.

Where to Try Churros:

For over **85 years**, **Casa Aranda** has been Málaga's go-to place for **churros con chocolate**. This traditional café is an institution in the city, known for serving **crispy, perfectly fried churros** alongside steaming cups of **thick, velvety hot chocolate**. The charming, old-fashioned setting and **friendly atmosphere** make it a must-visit for both locals and tourists

What to Expect:

- Fresh, hot churros served straight from the fryer.
- A friendly atmosphere where locals gather to enjoy their morning treat.

Where to Find Casa Aranda:

- **Address**: Calle Herrería del Rey, 3, 29005 Málaga, Spain.
- **Price Range**: Approximately €3 - €10 per person.
- **Opening Hours**: Daily, 8:00 AM – 1:45 PM / 4:30 PM – 8:15 PM.

2. Tortas de Aceite: Sweet Olive Oil Biscuits

Known for its artisanal baking techniques, La Canasta offers **handcrafted Tortas de Aceite** that are **perfectly crisp and delicately sweetened**, making them a local favorite. Their biscuits are made fresh daily using **extra virgin olive oil, sesame seeds, and a hint of anise**, following a traditional recipe passed down through generations.

Where to Try Tortas de Aceite:

Pastelería Casa Mira has been around since 1890 and is one of the best spots to grab a **torta de aceite**. Here, the pastries are baked fresh daily, ensuring that each bite is as crisp and flavorful as the last.

What to Expect:

- Crispy, slightly sweet pastries made with high-quality **olive oil**.

- A cozy bakery that's a local favorite.

Where to Find La Canasta:

- **Address**: Avenue de Cánovas del Castillo, 2, Málaga-Este, 29016 Málaga, Spain.

- **Website**: https://lacanasta.es/

- **Phone**: +34 664 60 93 08.

- **Price Range**: €2 - €10 per packet.

- **Opening Hours**: Daily, 8:00 AM – 11:00 PM.

3. Bocadillo de Jamón: The Perfect Sandwich

If you want to eat like a local, then you can't miss out on a **bocadillo de jamón**, a simple but satisfying sandwich made with **Spanish cured ham**. The bread is usually a soft baguette-style roll, and the ham is thinly sliced, rich in flavor, and often paired with a bit of **tomato** and **olive oil**. It's perfect for a quick snack or lunch.

Where to Try Bocadillo de Jamón:

Hidden in an alleyway near the historic center, **La Recova** is a cozy, rustic café known for its **traditional Andalusian breakfast and bocadillos**. Their **bocadillo de jamón** is made with **freshly baked bread** and generously filled with **hand-cut Jamón Serrano**, creating a perfect balance of flavor and texture. Pair it with a **cup of local coffee** for an authentic Spanish experience.

What to Expect:

- **Freshly sliced ham** paired with crunchy bread.
- A laid-back atmosphere where you can grab your sandwich and enjoy it on the go.

Where to Find La Recova:

- **Address**: Pasaje Nuestra Señora de los Dolores de San Juan, 5, 29005 Málaga, Spain
- **Phone**: +34 744 61 76 58.
- **Opening Hours**: Monday to Saturday 8:30AM – 3:00 PM, closed on Sundays.

- Approximately **€4 to €10** per person.

4. Pescaito Frito: Fried Fish at its Best

Another classic in **Malaga's street food scene** is **pescaito frito**, which translates to **fried fish**. This dish typically includes a variety of small fish, such as anchovies and squid, all battered and fried until crispy. It's often served in a cone or small paper bag, making it easy to enjoy while walking through the streets.

Where to Try Pescaito Frito:

Known for using **fresh, locally sourced fish**, Freidura Los Gatos serves some of the best **boquerones (anchovies), calamares (squid), and adobo (marinated fish)** in Málaga. The lively atmosphere and traditional Spanish decor make it a great place to experience authentic Andalusian cuisine.

What to Expect:

- Crispy, light batter with tender fish inside.
- A casual environment where locals come to grab their fried fish fix.

Where to Find Freidura Los Gatos:

- **Address**: Plaza Uncibay, 9, 29008 Málaga, Spain.
- **Phone**: +34 952 22 23 40.

- **Opening Hours:** Daily, 11:00 AM – 12:00 AM.

- **Price Range**: Approximately €10 to €20 per person.

5. Empanadas: Savory Pastries on the Go

If you're looking for a portable snack to munch on while exploring the streets, then try **empanadas**. These **savory pastries** are filled with various ingredients such as **tuna, chicken**, or **ham and cheese**. They're perfect for a quick lunch or snack while you're on the move.

Where to Try Empanadas:

La Martina Gastrotienda offers a variety of **homemade empanadas**, prepared with high-quality ingredients. Their menu includes **both traditional and creative flavors**, such as **caramelized onion & goat cheese, mushroom truffle, and spicy beef**. Located near Málaga's **Atarazanas Market**, it's a fantastic stop for a quick snack or to take some empanadas home for later.

What to Expect:

- **Freshly baked empanadas** with a golden, flaky crust.

- A variety of fillings to suit all tastes.

Where to Find La Empanada Malagueña:

- **Address**: Calle Sebastián Souvirón, 4, 29005 Málaga, Spain.

- **Phone**: +34 951 43 42 85.

- **Opening Hours:** Daily, 10:00 AM – 10:00 PM.

- **Price Range**: Approximately €2.50 - €5 per empanada.

Tips for Enjoying Street Food in Malaga:

- **Be Adventurous**: Don't be afraid to try something new. **Malaga's street food** is all about exploring different flavors and textures.

- **Cash Is King**: While some places accept cards, it's always a good idea to carry some **cash** with you when visiting street vendors.

- **Take Your Time**: Street food is meant to be enjoyed slowly, so find a spot to sit down and savor the flavors.

Malaga's **street food** scene is vibrant, delicious, and full of surprises. From **sweet churros** to **fried fish**, the city's culinary offerings are as rich and diverse as the culture itself. Make sure to stop by these local spots to get a true taste of what **Malaga** has to offer.

Seafood: A Taste of the Mediterranean

If you're lucky enough to find yourself in **Malaga**, you're in for a treat—especially if you're a fan of **seafood**. The city's location on the **Mediterranean coast** means that **fresh fish** and **seafood** are always on the menu. From bustling markets to intimate seaside restaurants, Malaga offers some of the best seafood you'll ever taste. In this chapter, we'll share our favorite spots where you can dive into the freshest and most flavorful **seafood** dishes.

1. Paella de Mariscos: The Ultimate Seafood Dish

When it comes to **Mediterranean seafood**, **paella** is the dish that steals the show. A classic Spanish **paella** is made with **seafood** like **shrimp**, **clams**, and **mussels**, all cooked together with **saffron rice** for a rich, flavorful meal. Although paella originated in **Valencia**, you can find amazing versions all over **Malaga**, particularly in the **chiringuitos** along the coast.

Where to Try Paella de Mariscos:

If you're looking for a **classic paella experience in the heart of Málaga, Los Mellizos Málaga** is an excellent choice. Known for its **expertly cooked rice dishes**, this restaurant serves **one of the most famous paellas de mariscos** in the city. Their paella is made with **local seafood, homemade broth, and perfectly balanced saffron seasoning**, creating a **delicious and aromatic dish**.

What to Expect:

- A heaping portion of **seafood** mixed with fragrant **saffron rice**.

- A traditional dining experience where you can savor the flavors of the **Mediterranean**.

Where to Find Los Mellizos:

- **Address**: Calle Sancha de Lara, 7, 29015 Málaga, Spain**.**

- **Website:** www.losmellizos.net

- **Phone**: +34 952 22 03 15.

- **Opening Hours:** Daily, 1:00 PM – 11:00 PM.

- **Price Range**: Approximately €20 - €30 per person.

2. Gambas a la Plancha: Grilled Shrimp with a Twist

Gambas a la plancha, or **grilled shrimp**, is another must-try seafood dish in **Malaga**. The shrimp are seasoned simply with **olive oil**, **garlic**, and a squeeze of **lemon**, then grilled to perfection. The result is sweet, juicy shrimp with a smoky flavor that's hard to beat. Perfect for sharing or as an appetizer, **gambas a la plancha** can be found at many local restaurants and seafood bars.

Where to Try Gambas a la Plancha:

If you're looking for a more **relaxed, beachside experience**, **Chiringuito La Campana** is the perfect choice. Located right on the **Paseo Marítimo**, this **local favorite** serves up **delicious gambas a la plancha** grilled over an open flame, giving them that **perfect smoky flavor**. Sit back with **your feet in the sand**, enjoy the **ocean breeze**, and watch as the chefs prepare your shrimp **right in front of you**.

What to Expect:

- Sweet and smoky **grilled shrimp** that practically melt in your mouth.
- A relaxed environment where you can enjoy fresh seafood in good company.

Where to Find Chiringuito La Campana:

- **Address**: Paseo Marítimo Antonio Banderas, 29004 Málaga, Spain.
- **Phone**: +34 952 23 99 68.

- **Opening Hours**: 11:00 AM – 12:00 AM (Daily).
- **Price Range**: Approximately €15 - €30 per person.

3. Calamares: Tender Fried Squid Rings

If you've never had **calamares** (fried squid), you're in for a treat. This dish features tender rings of squid coated in **light batter** and fried to golden perfection. It's one of **Malaga's** most popular seafood dishes, and you can find it all over the city, from **beachside stalls** to **fancy restaurants**.

Where to Try Calamares:

For a **classic, no-frills tapas experience**, **La Campana** is a must-visit. Tucked away in the historic center of Málaga, this small but lively **traditional tavern** has been serving some of the best calamares in town for decades. Their **light, crunchy batter** and **fresh, tender squid** make their fried squid rings a local favorite.

What to Expect:

- Lightly battered, crispy squid with a tender, juicy center.
- An authentic **Malagan** dining experience with a variety of local dishes.

Where to Find La Campana:

- **Address**: Calle Granada, 35, 29015 Málaga, Spain.
- **Website**: https://www.lacampanamalaga.es/
- **Price Range**: Approximately €10 - €30 per person.
- **Opening Hours:** Monday to Saturday 12:30 PM – 4:00 PM, 8:00 PM – 12:00 PM, (Open from 12:30 PM – 4:00 PM on Sundays).

4. Boquerones: Anchovies in Vinegar

One of **Malaga's** most iconic seafood dishes is **boquerones en vinagre**—fresh **anchovies** marinated in **vinegar** and **garlic**. The dish is simple, but it packs a punch in terms of flavor. You'll often see it served with a drizzle of **olive oil** and a few **parsley** leaves on top. It's a light, refreshing way to enjoy the fresh fish of the region.

Where to Try Boquerones en Vinagre:

Located right by the beach, this lively **chiringuito** (beach bar) is famous for its **auction-style service**, where waiters walk around announcing the dishes they have, and you simply raise your hand to claim your plate. Their **boquerones en vinagre** are a crowd favorite—**tender, citrusy, and served with fresh bread**.

What to Expect:

- Tangy, fresh anchovies with a hint of **garlic** and a dash of **olive oil**.

- A lively, local spot to enjoy a bite of authentic **Malaga** seafood.

Where to Find El Tintero:

- **Address**: Avenida Salvador Allende, 340, 29017 Málaga, Spain.

- **Website**: https://eltinteromalaga.com/
- **Phone**: +34 650 68 09 56.

- **Price Range**: Approximately €20 - €30 per person.

- **Opening Hours:** 12:30 PM – 11:30 PM (Daily).

Tips for Enjoying Seafood in Malaga:

- **Ask for the Daily Catch**: Many restaurants serve fresh **seafood** based on the day's catch, so don't hesitate to ask what's available.

- **Savor Slowly**: Mediterranean seafood is meant to be enjoyed slowly, so take your time and appreciate the fresh flavors.

- **Pair with Wine**: **Malaga** has fantastic **local wines**, so don't forget to ask your server for recommendations to pair with your seafood.

Whether you're savoring **grilled sardines**, **fried squid**, or a classic **paella**, **Malaga's seafood** scene offers a taste of the **Mediterranean** like no other. Each bite is a reflection of the region's rich maritime culture, and every dish tells a story of the sea.

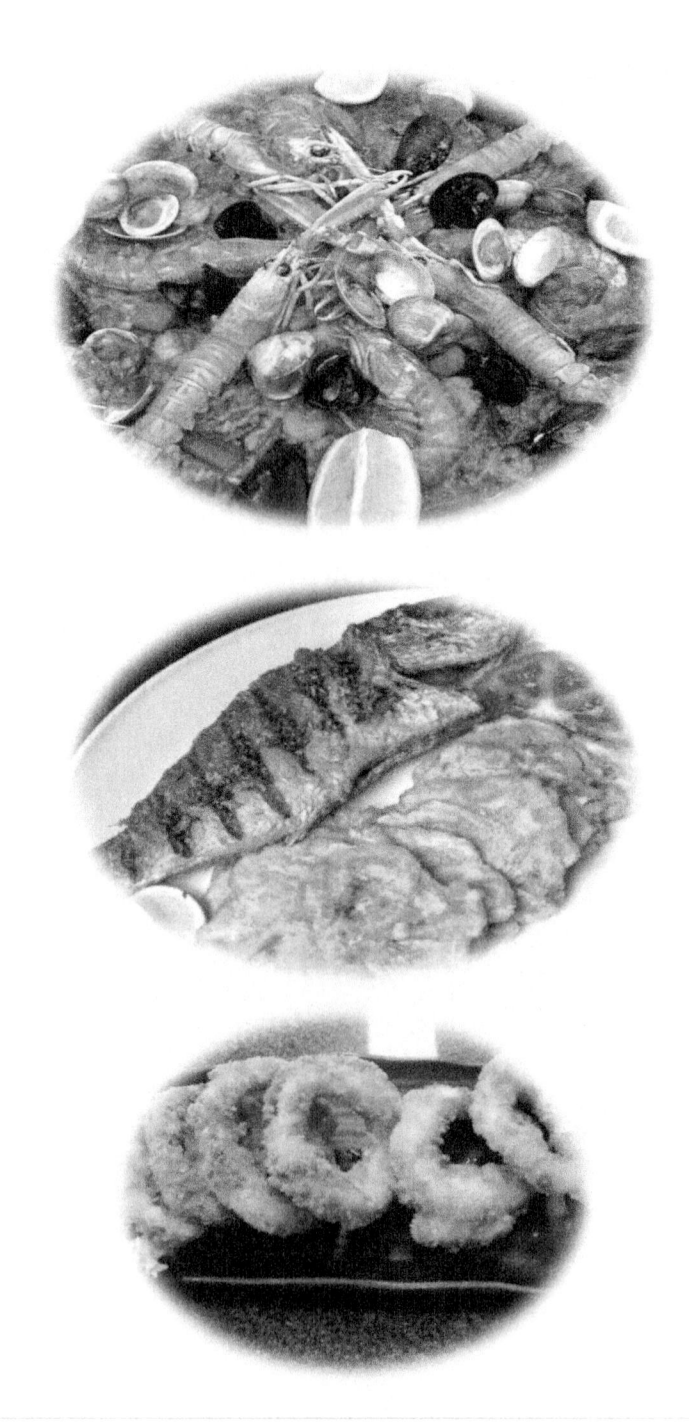

150 | MALAGA TRAVEL GUIDE 2025

Chapter 6

Málaga's Cultural Festivals and Traditions

Málaga is a city that thrives on its **rich cultural traditions and vibrant celebrations**, offering visitors a glimpse into the soul of Andalusia. From the solemn processions of **Semana Santa (Holy Week)** to the lively streets of the **Feria de Agosto**, and from the artistic energy of the **Málaga Film Festival** to the heartfelt rhythms of **flamenco and live music**, this chapter explores the events that make Málaga's cultural calendar so captivating. These festivals and traditions are not just celebrations; they are a reflection of the city's identity and its people's passion for life, art, and heritage.

Semana Santa (Holy Week): A Deep Dive into Malaga's Traditions

If you're lucky enough to visit **Malaga** during **Semana Santa** (Holy Week), you're in for an experience like no other. This annual celebration is one of the city's most important traditions, and it's a time when **Malaga** truly comes alive with passion, history, and religious devotion. In this section, we will take you through the rich cultural heritage and stunning processions that make **Semana Santa** in **Malaga** so unique.

What is Semana Santa?

Semana Santa, or **Holy Week**, is the week leading up to **Easter Sunday** in Spain. It's a deeply religious time, celebrated with processions, rituals, and displays of devotion throughout the country. But in **Malaga, Semana Santa** takes on a particularly unique and dramatic flair.

In **Malaga**, the week is marked by **processions** that take place on the streets, where people gather to watch religious brotherhoods (called **cofradías**) carry massive, ornately decorated floats, known as **pasos**, through the city. These floats often feature **religious images** such as **Jesus**, **Mary**, or **the saints**, and they are carried by **penitents** dressed in traditional **robes** and **conical hats**. The processions are accompanied by haunting **saeta** songs, **drums**, and **cymbals**, all creating a powerful atmosphere.

The Processions: A Spectacle of Faith and Passion

The **Semana Santa** processions in **Malaga** are famous for their emotional intensity and unique style. The **pasos** are carried by **costaleros**, men who carry the floats on their shoulders, while the **nazarenos**, penitents who wear long robes and pointed hoods, walk along the streets in a solemn, almost meditative manner. This combination of faith and performance makes **Malaga's Semana Santa** one of the most visually striking in all of Spain.

Key Processions to Watch:

La Hermandad del Rico (The Brotherhood of the Rich)
One of the most famous processions in **Malaga**, **La Hermandad del Rico** is known for its **unique tradition**: the **"Christ of the Good Death"** is carried through the streets on the shoulders of the brotherhood, and as it passes, **the faithful kneel and pray**. This procession is one of the most deeply moving processions of the week.

What to Expect:

- A beautiful **religious float** of **Christ** on the cross.
- Solemnity and reverence as the procession makes its way through the streets.

Where to See the Procession:

- **Location**: The procession begins at **Iglesia de San Felipe Neri** and makes its way through the **historic center** of **Malaga**.
- **Date**: The procession typically takes place on **Maundy Thursday (Jueves Santo)**, which falls on the Thursday before Easter.

La Hermandad de los Estudiantes (The Brotherhood of the Students)

This is one of the most **spectacular** processions, as it features a **float** of the **Virgen de la Esperanza** and is known for its **elegant** and **dignified procession**. The procession is highly anticipated by both locals and visitors alike.

What to Expect:

- Beautiful **flower arrangements** adorning the float.
- A slow and graceful procession, accompanied by traditional **religious music**.

Where to See the Procession:

- **Location**: The procession starts at **Iglesia de los Estudiantes** and winds through **Calle de Carretería** and other central streets in **Malaga**.
- **Date: Good Friday (Viernes Santo)** is the key day for this procession, one of the most significant of **Semana Santa**.

The Traditions and Customs of Semana Santa

The Penitents

One of the most striking aspects of **Semana Santa** in **Malaga** is the presence of **nazarenos**—penitents who dress in long robes and pointed hoods, called **capirotes**. They participate in the processions as a sign of devotion, and their participation is deeply rooted in centuries-old traditions. These **nazarenos** walk in **solemn silence**, some carrying candles, while others perform acts of **penance**.

The Saetas: Songs of Passion

As the processions make their way through the streets, the powerful **saeta** songs fill the air. These songs are often sung spontaneously from balconies as the processions pass below. The **saeta** is a hauntingly beautiful, flamenco-style song that expresses the deep religious fervor of the singers. It's one of the most emotional and memorable experiences during **Semana Santa**.

The Costaleros

Behind each **paso**, there are groups of **costaleros**, men who carry the floats on their shoulders. These **costaleros** are part of a centuries-old tradition and carry the **pasos** with great skill and devotion. The **costaleros** are often seen as heroes of **Semana Santa**, as they bear the heavy floats through the streets, sometimes for hours, while maintaining their balance and dignity.

Where to Stay During Semana Santa

If you're planning to visit **Malaga** during **Semana Santa**, it's a good idea to book your accommodations well in advance, as the city gets very busy during this time. Many hotels offer special **Semana Santa packages**, so make sure to check for **deals**.

Recommended Hotel:

Hotel Sur Málaga

A budget-friendly hotel with easy access to **historic Malaga** and close to the action during **Semana Santa** processions. The hotel is known for its warm hospitality and comfortable rooms, making it the perfect base for exploring the city.

- **Address**: Calle Trinidad Grund, 13, 29001 Málaga, Spain.
- **Website**: https://www.hotel-sur.com/
- **Phone**: +34 952 22 48 00.
- **Price Range**: Approximately **€60 to €120** per night.
- **Opening Hours**: 24-hour reception.

Eating During Semana Santa

During **Semana Santa**, **Malaga** is filled with special **traditional foods** that are only available during this time. From **torrijas**

(Spanish-style French toast) to **potajes** (hearty stews), you'll have plenty of local treats to enjoy.

Where to Try Torrijas:

Casa Aranda

A local institution that serves up some of the best **torrijas** in the city, perfect for sweet-toothed visitors.

- **Address**: Calle de Herrería del Rey, 3, 29005 Málaga, Spain.
- **Price Range:** Approximately €3 - €10 per person.
- **Opening Hours**: Daily, 8:00 AM – 1:45 PM / 4:30 PM – 8:15 PM.

A Word of Advice for Visitors

- **Plan Ahead**: During **Semana Santa**, **Malaga** gets crowded, so it's best to plan ahead for everything—from accommodations to where you'll eat. Make sure to book your tickets for attractions early, as many places close or have limited hours during **Holy Week**.
- **Respect the Traditions**: **Semana Santa** is a time of deep religious significance, so be respectful of the processions and the devotion of the locals. If you're not sure about something, don't hesitate to ask a local or a member of the brotherhood.

There's no other time of the year quite like **Semana Santa** in **Malaga**. The city is transformed into a living, breathing expression of faith, passion, and tradition. Whether you're witnessing the processions firsthand, listening to a **saeta**, or simply soaking in the atmosphere, this is an experience you won't forget. It's a celebration of life, faith, and the deep-rooted traditions that have shaped **Malaga** for centuries.

Feria de Agosto: Malaga's Summer Fair and Party

If you're visiting **Malaga** in **August**, you're in for a treat! The **Feria de Agosto**, or **Malaga Summer Fair**, is one of the biggest and most exciting events of the year. It's a vibrant celebration of **local culture**, **tradition**, and **fun** that draws both locals and visitors from all over the world. This chapter will take you through what makes this fair such a unique experience and give you all the details you need to fully enjoy the festivities.

What is Feria de Agosto?

The **Feria de Agosto** is **Malaga's annual summer fair**, held every August to celebrate the city's patron saint, **Our Lady of the Victories** (La Virgen de la Victoria). It dates back to the **19th century** and has grown into a massive event that lasts for an entire week. During this time, the city bursts with life, as locals and tourists flock to the **fairgrounds**, **streets**, and **squares** to enjoy music, dancing, food, and countless activities.

Whether you're into **traditional Andalusian music, flamenco dancing**, or simply love the idea of eating and drinking your way through one of Spain's biggest parties, **Feria de Agosto** has something for everyone.

Key Attractions at Feria de Agosto

1. The Fairground (Recinto Ferial)

The **Recinto Ferial** is the **beating heart** of **Feria de Agosto**, transforming into a **spectacular world of lights, music, and celebration** each year. Located just outside Málaga's city center, this **massive fairground** is where locals and visitors alike come together to enjoy the **ultimate festival experience**. As night falls, the fairground bursts into life, with **colorful decorations, thrilling rides, and lively casetas (marquee tents)** filling the space with an **electric energy**.

What to Expect:

- **Amusement Rides**: Roller coasters, Ferris wheels, and other classic fair attractions.
- **Street Performers**: Musicians, dancers, and entertainers adding to the lively vibe.
- **Food Stalls**: Indulge in **local delicacies** like **churros with chocolate, fried fish, and jamón ibérico**, as well as classic **fair snacks** like cotton candy.
- **Fireworks & Light Displays:** Every evening, the sky lights up with **spectacular fireworks**, adding to the magic of the festival.

Where to See It:

- **Location**: Recinto Ferial de Málaga, Calle Antonio Rodríguez Sánchez, 29006 Málaga, Spain.
- **Opening Hours**: The fairground opens **every evening** from around **8:00 PM until late**, typically from **August 15th to August 20th**.
- **Entry**: **Entry:** Free entrance, but **rides, food, and attractions** may have individual costs.

2. Flamenco Dancing and Live Music

No celebration in **Malaga** would be complete without some **flamenco**! During **Feria de Agosto**, there are countless performances of **flamenco music and dancing** that showcase the soul of Andalusia. The energy and passion of **flamenco** are truly captivating, and you'll likely find yourself tapping your feet or even joining in if you're up for it.

What to Expect:

- **Flamenco Shows**: Enjoy **live performances** at various venues throughout the fair. Some shows are free, while others may have a small entry fee.
- **Traditional Music**: Hear the sounds of the **guitar**, **castanets**, and **cante jondo**, the deep and soulful singing that makes flamenco so special.

Where to See It:

- **Location**: Throughout Málaga's city center and Recinto Ferial, with performances in casetas and public squares like **Plaza de la Constitución** and **Calle Larios**.
- **Opening Hours**: Flamenco shows and live music performances take place throughout the day and night, from **August 15th to August 20th**.
- **Entry**: Free for most public performances.

3. The Parade of the Fair (El Pregón de la Feria)

The **official kickoff** to the **Feria de Agosto** is **El Pregón de la Feria**, a large-scale **opening parade** that marks the beginning of Málaga's most anticipated celebration. This grand event, held on the **first night of the feria**, brings together thousands of spectators as they gather to witness a **colorful procession**, fireworks, and live music. The parade is led by the **Pregonero**, an honorary figure chosen each year to give the **opening speech**, setting the tone for the week-long festivities.

What to Expect:

- **Parade Floats**: Beautifully decorated **floats** carrying figures of **the patron saint** and other **religious symbols**.

- **Traditional Costumes**: Expect to see many people dressed in the traditional **traje de flamenca**, a colorful dress worn by women during celebrations.

Where to See It:

- **Location**: The parade moves through Málaga's historic center, typically beginning at **Avenida de Cervantes** and continuing toward the **Málaga Port**.
- **Opening Hours**: The event takes place on the **evening before the feria officially begins**, usually around **10:00 PM**.
- **Entry**: Free for all spectators.

Food and Drink at Feria de Agosto

You can't talk about a Spanish fair without mentioning **food and drink**. During **Feria de Agosto**, food is everywhere! From the classic **tapas** to **fried fish**, you'll find a huge variety of delicious bites to enjoy.

Must-Try Foods:

- **Fried Fish (Pescaíto Frito)**: A **Malaga** classic. Fresh fish, battered and fried to perfection, served with a squeeze of **lemon**.

- **Tortillas de Patatas**: Spanish omelets, often made with **potatoes**, **onions**, and **eggs**.
- **Churros con Chocolate**: Fried dough, served with a thick, rich **chocolate sauce**.

Where to Try It:

Chiringuito El Cachalote

A beachfront restaurant perfect for trying **pescaíto frito** and other fresh seafood. Enjoy a meal by the sea while soaking in the lively atmosphere of **Malaga**.

- **Address**: Calle Litoral, 29017 Málaga, Spain.
- **Website**: www.chiringuitoelcachalote.com
- **Phone**: +34 627 86 37 23.
- **Price Range:** Approximately €20 - €30 per person.

Where to Stay During Feria de Agosto

Since **Feria de Agosto** is a major event in **Malaga**, it's best to book your accommodations early, as hotels fill up quickly. Here's a great place to stay if you want to be close to the action.

Recommended Hotel:

Hotel Sur Málaga

Located just a short distance from the **Recinto Ferial**, this hotel offers comfortable rooms and easy access to all the festivities.

Tips for Enjoying Feria de Agosto

- **Wear Comfortable Shoes**: There's a lot of walking and dancing, so make sure you bring shoes that are both stylish and comfortable.

- **Stay Hydrated**: It can get quite hot in **Malaga** during August, so drink plenty of water between your **frozen sangrias** and **tapas**.

- **Embrace the Culture**: Take part in the festivities by wearing a **flamenco-style dress** or **bright, festive clothing**.

If you're in **Malaga** during **Feria de Agosto**, get ready to experience one of the most exciting celebrations in Spain! From the **fairgrounds** and **flamenco performances** to the **traditional food** and **lively parades**, this is a festival you don't want to miss.

Malaga Film Festival: A Celebration of Cinema

Malaga Film Festival: A Celebration of Cinema

The **Málaga Film Festival (Festival de Málaga)** is one of Spain's most important **cinema events**, dedicated to celebrating **Spanish and Latin American films**. Established in **1998**, this annual festival transforms the city into a hub for **filmmakers, actors, and movie enthusiasts**. With a packed schedule of **film screenings, red carpet events, industry panels, and award ceremonies**, the festival plays a crucial role in promoting **Spanish-language cinema on the international stage**.

We will take you through everything you need to know about the **Malaga Film Festival**, including the best places to watch films, where to spot celebrities, and how to make the most of your visit.

What is the Malaga Film Festival?

The **Malaga Film Festival** started in **1998** and has since become one of the most important film festivals in Spain. It focuses on **Spanish and Latin American cinema**, helping new directors, actors, and filmmakers showcase their work.

For ten days, Malaga turns into a **Hollywood-style** city with red carpets, film premieres, and celebrity sightings. It's an amazing time to visit, whether you love **watching movies**, **meeting filmmakers**, or just enjoying the electric atmosphere.

When and Where is the Festival?

- **Date**: Usually held in **March or April** (exact dates vary each year).

Main Venues:

- **Teatro Cervantes** (the main cinema for premieres and gala events).
- **Teatro Echegaray** (a smaller, more intimate venue).
- **Albéniz Cinema** (great for watching festival films in a relaxed setting).
- **Plaza de la Merced** (outdoor screenings and events).

Key Highlights of the Festival

1. The Red Carpet at Teatro Cervantes

The **Teatro Cervantes Red Carpet** is one of the most anticipated events of the **Málaga Film Festival**, drawing actors, directors, and film enthusiasts from across Spain and beyond. As the **epicenter of the festival**, the red carpet transforms the area around **Teatro Cervantes** into a showcase of cinematic talent, fashion, and media coverage. Attendees gather to witness **celebrities arriving**, photographers capturing iconic moments, and interviews taking place before the screenings.

- **Where to Go**: The best place to spot celebrities is **outside Teatro Cervantes** before a big premiere.

Where to See It:

- **Location**: Teatro Cervantes, Calle Ramos Marín, 1, 29012 Málaga, Spain
- **Opening Hours**: The red carpet is typically active in the early evening, during the **Málaga Film Festival** (held annually in March).
- **Entry**: Public viewing is free, but access to film screenings and gala events requires tickets.
- **Website**: https://www.teatrocervantes.com/

2. Film Screenings at Albéniz Cinema

Albéniz Cinema is a key location for film enthusiasts in Málaga, offering a mix of **international films, Spanish cinema, and independent productions**. Located in the **historic center**, this theater is known for hosting **special screenings, film festivals, and classic retrospectives** throughout the year. It plays a significant role in Málaga's **cinematic culture**, particularly as a main venue for the **Málaga Film Festival**.

What to Expect:

- Festival films are shown throughout the day.
- Some screenings include **Q&A sessions** with directors and actors.
- Tickets are **affordable**, so you can watch multiple films.

Where to See It:

Cine Albéniz

- **Address**: Calle Alcazabilla, 4, 29015 Málaga, Spain.
- **Opening Hours**: Open daily, with screenings typically from **4:00 PM to midnight**.
- **Entry**: Ticket prices vary depending on the film, with discounts available for students and seniors.
- **Website**: www.cinealbeniz.com
- **Phone**: +34 951 57 11 13.

3. Open-Air Screenings at Plaza de la Merced

One of the best parts of the **Malaga Film Festival** is the **outdoor screenings** at **Plaza de la Merced**. This is where you can watch **classic Spanish films** or festival selections **under the stars**. It's a fantastic experience, especially with the **Malaga Cathedral** lit up in the background.

What to Expect:

- Free film screenings every evening.

- A lively atmosphere with **locals and tourists** enjoying the films.

- Food stalls selling **popcorn, snacks, and drinks**.

Where to See It:

- **Location:** Plaza de la Merced, 29012 Málaga, Spain.
- **Opening Hours:** Screenings typically begin **at sunset** and continue into the night throughout the duration of the festival.
- **Entry:** Free admission; seating is available on a first-come, first-served basis.
- **Website:** https://visita.malaga.eu/

4. The Golden Biznaga Awards Ceremony

The **Golden Biznaga Awards Ceremony** is the pinnacle event of the **Málaga Film Festival**, celebrating excellence in Spanish-language cinema. Recognized as one of Spain's most significant film industry events, the ceremony brings together **directors, actors, producers, and film enthusiasts** to honor outstanding achievements in filmmaking. The **Biznaga de Oro (Golden**

Biznaga) is the festival's highest award, named after Málaga's iconic jasmine flower.

What to Expect:

- **Award Presentations** – Prestigious accolades for categories such as **Best Film, Best Director, Best Screenplay, and Best Actor/Actress**.
- **Red Carpet Arrivals** – Spanish and international cinema stars arrive at the ceremony, offering a chance to witness high-profile moments.
- **Exclusive Screenings** – Special previews of award-winning films, providing an opportunity to see them before their wider release.

Where to See It:

- The awards ceremony takes place at **Teatro Cervantes** on the last day of the festival.
- **Entry**: Invitation-only event, but some public screenings and festival passes grant access.

Where to Stay During the Film Festival

Since **March and April** are busy months in **Malaga**, it's best to book your hotel early. Here are two great options depending on your budget:

Luxury Stay: Gran Hotel Miramar

If you want a luxurious experience, this **5-star hotel** is one of the best in Malaga. Many **celebrities** also stay here during the festival.

Budget Stay: Hotel Sur Málaga

A great option for budget travelers. It's also comfortable and located near the main festival venues.

Where to Eat Near the Festival Venues

You'll definitely get hungry between movie screenings, so here are some great spots to grab a meal:

El Pimpi

This is one of **Malaga's most famous restaurants**, known for its **amazing tapas and local wines**. It's also a popular spot for celebrities during the festival.

If you want something quick and delicious, check out the **Atarazanas Market**. You'll find **fresh seafood, Spanish ham, and traditional Andalusian dishes**.

- **Address**: Calle Atarazanas, 10, 29005 Málaga, Spain.

- **Opening Hours**: Monday to Saturday, 9:00 AM – 2:00 PM.

Tips for Enjoying the Malaga Film Festival

- **Buy Tickets Early** – Popular films and events **sell out quickly**, so book in advance.

- **Dress Smart for Premieres** – If you're attending a **red-carpet event**, it's best to **dress up a little**.

- **Follow the Festival Schedule** – Check the official website for **film times and locations**.

- **Explore the City** – In between films, take some time to visit Malaga's top attractions like **Picasso Museum, Malaga Cathedral**, and **La Malagueta Beach**.

The **Málaga Film Festival** is an essential event for anyone passionate about **Spanish and Latin American cinema**. From **premiere screenings and outdoor movies to industry workshops and red-carpet events**, the festival offers a **comprehensive film experience** that celebrates **storytelling, creativity, and the future of filmmaking**. Whether you're a serious film fan or just love the excitement of a big cultural event, you'll love the energy of the festival. From red carpet premieres to outdoor screenings, there's something for everyone. So, grab your popcorn, find a great seat, and enjoy the best of **Spanish and Latin American cinema** in the heart of **Malaga**!

Flamenco and Live Music: Experience the Soul of Andalusia

If you want to feel the **true spirit of Andalusia**, there's nothing like **Flamenco**. It's not just music or dance—it's **raw emotion, passion, and storytelling** all in one. The rhythm of the guitar, the power of the singer's voice, and the intensity of the dancer's movements all come together to create something **unforgettable**.

And Malaga? It's one of the **best places in Spain** to experience Flamenco in its **purest form**. From **intimate Flamenco bars** to **grand tablaos**, there are plenty of places to **soak in the magic** of live music.

What is Flamenco?

Flamenco is a **deeply emotional** art form that originated in **Andalusia**, combining **singing (cante)**, **guitar playing (toque)**, and **dancing (baile)**. It was born from **a mix of cultures**, including **Gypsy, Moorish, Jewish, and Spanish influences**, making it **one of the richest traditions in the world**.

Flamenco is all about **duende**—a Spanish word that describes the deep **spiritual and emotional connection** between the artist and the audience. You don't just **listen** to Flamenco; you **feel** it!

Where to Experience Flamenco in Malaga

Malaga has some of **the best Flamenco venues** in Spain. Whether you want an **authentic, local vibe** or a **high-energy performance**, there's something for everyone.

1. Peña Juan Breva – The Most Authentic Flamenco Experience

Flamenco in Málaga wouldn't be the same without **Peña Juan Breva**, a cultural institution that has been dedicated to **traditional flamenco performances and education since 1958**. This venue was named after **Juan Breva**, one of Málaga's most celebrated flamenco singers, and continues to honor his legacy by showcasing **some of the best flamenco artists in Spain**. Unlike tourist-focused tablaos, this space is known for its **deep commitment to flamenco's historic roots**, making it one of the most **genuine places to experience the art form**.

What to Expect:

- Authentic **cante jondo (deep singing)** performances.
- **Small, intimate setting**—perfect for feeling the emotion up close.

- A museum showcasing **Flamenco guitars, costumes, and historic photos**.

Where to See It:

- **Address**: Calle Ramón Franquelo, 4, 29008 Málaga, Spain.
- **Opening Hours**: Typically open for **evening performances** and special events. Check the official schedule for showtimes.
- **Entry**: Some performances are free, while special events sometimes require an entry fee. Reservations are recommended.
- **Phone**: +34 952 22 13 80.
- **Website**: https://xn--peajuanbreva-bhb.eu/

2. Tablao Alegría – A Stunning Flamenco Show with Dinner

Tablao Alegría is a **renowned Flamenco venue** where skilled performers take the stage in a setting designed to showcase the **intensity and artistry of Flamenco**. Located near Málaga's **port and historic center**, the venue offers nightly performances accompanied by a menu of classic Spanish dishes, making it an ideal spot for an immersive cultural experience.

What to Expect:

- A **professional Flamenco show** with some of the **best dancers and musicians**.

- A **restaurant serving traditional Spanish dishes** like **paella and tapas**.

- An **outdoor terrace** with great views of the city.

Where to See It:

- **Address**: Calle Vélez Málaga, 6, 29016 Málaga, Spain.

- **Opening Hours**: Shows typically start at **7:00 PM and 9:30 PM**, with dining available before or after the performance.

- **Entry**: Ticket prices range from **€25 to €60**, depending on the seating and dining package.

- **Phone**: +34 951 47 44 93.

- **Website**: https://flamencomalaga.com/

3. Kelipé – The Most Intense Flamenco Experience

Flamenco at **Kelipé** is an **unfiltered and deeply expressive** performance, showcasing the passion and precision of this Andalusian tradition. The venue is dedicated to preserving the **purity of Flamenco**, offering a **close and intimate** setting where every movement, strum, and vocal expression resonates with the audience. Unlike tourist-driven shows, Kelipé focuses on **genuine artistry**, performed by **seasoned Flamenco dancers, singers, and guitarists** who have dedicated their lives to this art.

What to Expect:

- A raw, emotional performance—you'll feel every beat of the music.
- Highly skilled dancers and musicians, performing in a small, intimate setting.
- A focus on traditional Flamenco, without the touristy feel.

Where to See It:

- **Address**: Calle Muro de Puerta Nueva, 10, 29005 Málaga, Spain.
- **Opening Hours**: Shows typically begin at 8:30 PM, but it is recommended to arrive early to secure seating.
- **Entry**: Ticket prices range from **€20 to €40**, depending on seating and availability.
- **Phone**: +34 665 09 73 59.
- **Website**: https://www.kelipe.net/

Where to Enjoy Live Music in Malaga

Malaga is not just about Flamenco—there's also a **vibrant live music scene** with everything from **jazz and blues** to **rock and indie bands**. Here are some of the best places to catch a live music show.

1. ZZ Pub – The Best Rock & Blues Bar in Malaga

For those who appreciate **live rock and blues music, ZZ Pub** is one of Málaga's top venues to experience an energetic night out. Located in the **city center**, this intimate music bar has been hosting **live performances** from local and international bands for decades. The venue's laid-back atmosphere and commitment to quality music make it a favorite among **rock and blues fans**.

What to Expect:

- Live rock, blues, and indie bands every night.
- A laid-back atmosphere with cheap drinks.
- Open until late, making it a great place to end the night.

Where to See It:

- **Address**: Calle Tejón y Rodríguez, 6, 29008 Málaga, Spain.
- **Phone**: +34 952 22 69 22.

- **Opening Hours**: Open nightly from 10:00 PM to 4:00 AM.
- **Entry**: Free, but some events require a cover charge.
- **Website**: www.zzpub.es

2. The Clarence Jazz Club – The Best Jazz Bar in Malaga

For those who appreciate **live jazz music, The Clarence Jazz Club** in Málaga is an excellent spot to experience outstanding performances in an intimate setting. This venue hosts **local and international jazz musicians**, offering a diverse lineup that ranges from **classic jazz and blues to swing and Latin jazz.**

What to Expect:

o Live jazz, soul, and funk music in a stylish setting.

o A wide selection of cocktails and Spanish wines.

o A friendly, welcoming vibe—great for jazz lovers.

Where to See It:

- **Address**: Calle Danza Invisible, 8, 29620 Torremolinos, Málaga, Spain.
- **Phone**: +34 951 91 80 87.
- **Opening Hours**: Typically open from **Wednesday to Saturday, 8:00 PM to 2:00 PM.**

- **Entry**: Ticket prices range from **€10 to €20** depending on the artist.

Whether you want to experience the **soul of Flamenco** or discover **Malaga's live music scene**, this city has something for every music lover.

From the **intensity of Flamenco** to the **relaxed vibe of jazz and blues**, Malaga is a place where music comes alive. So, grab a drink, find a great seat, and let the rhythm of **Andalusia** take over.

Chapter 7

Exploring Málaga's Shopping Scene

Málaga offers a diverse shopping experience that caters to every taste, from **traditional Andalusian crafts** to **modern fashion** and upscale retail destinations. Whether you're exploring the **local markets** for handmade souvenirs, browsing **boutiques** for unique fashion pieces, or visiting iconic Spanish department stores, Málaga provides endless opportunities to discover something special. This chapter will guide you through the best places to shop, highlighting **authentic local products**, **stylish malls**, and **exciting shopping streets** to make the most of your retail adventure.

Souvenir Shopping: Local Crafts and Products

Bringing home, a **piece of Malaga** is one of the best ways to remember your trip. Whether it's **handmade ceramics, olive oil, wine, or traditional Andalusian textiles**, Malaga is full of amazing local products that make perfect souvenirs. Forget the mass-produced keychains and fridge magnets—this section will help you find **authentic, high-quality** souvenirs that truly capture the **spirit of Malaga**.

What to Buy in Malaga

1. Ceramics – Traditional Andalusian Art

Malaga is famous for its **beautiful ceramics**, inspired by Moorish and Andalusian designs. You'll find plates, bowls, and tiles with **vibrant blue, green, and yellow patterns**—a perfect addition to any home.

📍 **Where to Buy:**

Cerámica Santa Ana

- **What They Offer:** Hand-painted plates, decorative pottery, and ceramic tile art.
- **Address:** Calle San Agustín, 19, 29015 Málaga, Spain.
- **Website:** www.ceramicasantaana.com
- **Price Range**: Approximately **€15 to €120** depending on the item.

2. Olive Oil – The Liquid Gold of Andalusia

Andalusian **olive oil** is some of the **best in the world**, and Malaga produces **high-quality extra virgin olive oil** that makes a great souvenir. Look for **cold-pressed, organic varieties** for the best flavor.

📍 **Where to Buy:**

La Chinata Malaga

- **What They Offer:** A wide selection of **olive oils,** olive-based gourmet foods, **cosmetics, and gourmet products** made from olives.

- **Address:** Calle Nueva, 7, 29005 Málaga, Spain.

- **Website:** www.lachinata.es

- **Price Range**: Approximately **€5 to €80** per item.

3. Local Wines – The Flavors of Malaga

Malaga is known for its **sweet wines**, made from the Moscatel grape. These wines have been enjoyed for centuries and make a perfect gift for wine lovers.

📍 **Where to Buy:**

Quitapenas Bodega

- **What They Offer:** High-quality Malaga wines with **over 140 years of tradition**.

- **Address:** Ctra. Guadalmar, 12, Churriana, 29004 Málaga, Spain.

- **Phone**: +34 952 24 75 95.

- **Price Range**: Approximately **€50 to €100+** per item.

- **Website:** www.quitapenas.es

4. Esparto Grass Crafts – Handmade Baskets and Decorations

Esparto grass weaving is an **ancient Andalusian tradition**, and you'll find **handmade baskets, rugs, and wall hangings** made by skilled artisans.

📍 **Where to Buy:**

Artesanía Morales

- **What They Offer:** Handmade **baskets, lampshades, rugs, and decorative esparto pieces**.

- **Address:** Calle San Juan, 18, 29005 Málaga, Spain.

- **Price Range:** Approximately **€50 to €100+** per item.

- **Website:** www.artesaniamorales.com

5. Spanish Fans and Shawls – Traditional Fashion

Spanish **hand-painted fans** (abanicos) and embroidered shawls (mantones) are timeless souvenirs that add a touch of **elegance and tradition** to any wardrobe.

📍 **Where to Buy:**

Abanicos Carbonell

- **What They Offer:** Hand-painted Spanish fans with beautiful **floral and artistic designs**.

- **Address:** Calle Nueva, 8, 29005 Málaga, Spain.

- **Price Range**: Approximately **€30 to €100+**, depending on the materials and craftsmanship

- **Website:** www.abanicoscarbonell.com

Best Shopping Streets and Markets in Malaga

If you prefer to **wander and explore**, Malaga has **great shopping areas** filled with local products. Here are some top picks:

Calle Marqués de Larios – The Main Shopping Street

This is Malaga's most famous shopping street, lined with boutiques, craft stores, and souvenir shops.

- 📍 **Location:** Calle Marqués de Larios, 29005 Málaga, Spain

Mercado de Atarazanas – The Best Market for Local Products

For a **truly local experience**, visit this **historic market**. You'll find **fresh produce, spices, wine, and artisanal products**.

📍 **Location:** Calle Atarazanas, 10, 29005 Málaga, Spain.
📞 **Phone:** +34 951 92 60 10.

📍 **Website:** https://mercadomalaga.es/

When it comes to souvenirs, **skip the tourist traps** and bring home something truly **special from Malaga**. Whether it's a **beautiful ceramic plate, a bottle of fine wine, or an embroidered Spanish shawl**, these **local crafts and products** will remind you of your trip for years to come.

Fashion Boutiques and Andalusian Markets

Shopping in Andalusia is an **experience of color, tradition, and style**. Whether you're hunting for **luxurious designer pieces, handcrafted leather goods, or vibrant flamenco dresses**, Andalusia's fashion boutiques and local markets have something for everyone. In this guide, We'll take you through the **best places to shop,** from **high-end boutiques to lively street markets** where you can find one-of-a-kind treasures.

Fashion Boutiques: Where to Find Style in Andalusia

If you're looking for **chic, elegant, and uniquely Spanish fashion**, Andalusia's boutiques are full of **tailored suits, high-quality leather goods, and stylish dresses** inspired by the region's rich culture.

1. High-End Fashion Boutiques

- ♀ **Adolfo Domínguez** – Contemporary Spanish Fashion

- **What They Offer:** This boutique features **modern and minimalist designs** by renowned Spanish designer **Adolfo Domínguez.** Known for its focus on sustainable fashion and high-quality materials, the shop offers a range of **elegant apparel, leather bags, and accessories**.

- **Address:** Calle Marqués de Larios, 3, 29005 Málaga, Spain.

- 📞 **Phone:** +34 900 333 717.

- **Opening Hours**: Monday to Saturday: 10:00 AM – 9:30 PM; Sunday: Closed

- 🌐 **Website:** www.adolfodominguez.com

📍 **Massimo Dutti** – Refined Elegance for Every Occasion

- **What They Offer:** Exclusive collections of clothing, shoes, and accessories, with an emphasis on fine tailoring and natural fabrics.

- **Address:** Calle Marqués de Larios, 9, 29015 Málaga, Spain.

- 📞 **Phone:** +34 951 17 17 47.

- **Opening Hours**: Monday to Saturday: 10:00 AM – 9:30 PM; Sunday: 12:00 PM – 9:00 PM.

- 🌐 **Website:** www.massimodutti.com

2. Local Flamenco and Traditional Boutiques

Lina Sevilla – *Flamenco Fashion House*

- **What They Offer:** Handcrafted **flamenco dresses, embroidered shawls, and traditional Andalusian accessories**.

- **Address:** Calle Álvarez Quintero, 11, Casco Antiguo, 41004 Sevilla, Spain.

- **Phone:** +34 608 33 88 81.

- **Website:** www.linasevilla.com

- **Opening Hours:** Monday to Friday, 10:30 AM – 8:00 PM; Saturday, 11:00 AM – 6:00 PM.

Moda Flamenca Mari Cruz – *Authentic Flamenco Style*

- **What They Offer:** Custom-made flamenco dresses, hand-painted fans, and Spanish accessories.

- **Address:** Plaza Chirinos, 1, Centro, 14001 Córdoba, Spain.

- **Phone:** +34 957 61 28 68.

- **Website:** https://maricruz.es/

- **Opening Hours**: Monday to Friday, 10:30 AM – 8:30 PM; Saturday, 10:00 AM – 2:00 PM.

3. Leather Goods & Handcrafted Shoes

Andalusia is famous for **high-quality leather goods**, especially from **Ubrique**, where artisans have been crafting **luxury leather bags, shoes, and wallets for centuries**.

📍 **Made in Málaga Leather Workshop**

- **What They Offer:** Custom-made leather shoes, handbags, and accessories.
- **Address:** Calle Esparteros, 9, 29005 Málaga, Spain.
- 🌐 **Website:** www.madeinmalaga.com
- **Opening Hours**: Monday to Saturday, 9:30 AM – 7:00 PM

Andalusian Markets: Where to Find Hidden Treasures

If you love browsing through stalls, discovering unique handmade goods, and bargaining with local vendors, Andalusia's lively markets are a must-visit.

1. Mercado de Triana – Seville's Most Famous Market

- **What to Find:** Handcrafted ceramics, traditional Andalusian textiles, fresh produce, and gourmet olive oil.

- **Location:** Calle San Jorge, 6, 41010 Sevilla, Spain.

- 📞 **Phone:** +34 674 07 40 99.

- **Website**: www.mercadodetriana.com

- **Opening Hours:** Monday to Saturday: 8:00 AM – 3:00 PM.

2. Mercado Central de Atarazanas – The Best in Malaga

- **What to Find:** Local food products, artisanal goods, handmade crafts, and Andalusian fashion accessories.

- **Location:** Calle Atarazanas, 10, 29005 Málaga, Spain.

- 📞 **Phone:** +34 951 92 60 10.

3. Mercado de la Encarnación – The Jewel of Granada

- **What to Find:** Authentic flamenco accessories, vintage clothing, and unique leather goods.

- **Location:** Plaza de la Encarnación, 4, 18001 Granada, Spain.

- **Website:** https://mercadodelaencarnacion.es/

- **Opening Hours**: Monday to Saturday, 8:00 AM – 3:00 PM.

4. Mercado de Rastro – The Best Flea Market in Andalusia

- **What to Find:** Antique furniture, handmade Spanish jewelry, bohemian-style clothing, and rare collectibles.

- **Location:** Plaza de Cascorro, 28012 Madrid (popular Andalusian-style market in Spain).

- **Opening Hours:** Sundays, 9:00 AM – 3:00 PM.

Whether you're shopping for **luxury Andalusian fashion, handcrafted leather accessories, or vibrant flamenco dresses**, the **fashion boutiques and markets of Andalusia** offer something truly special. The key to finding the best pieces is to **explore small boutiques, visit family-run stores, and wander through local markets** where artisans sell their creations with **passion and pride**.

Wherever you choose to shop, you'll find something that not only reflects **Andalusia's rich culture and history** but also makes for a **timeless keepsake** from your journey.

El Corte Inglés: Spain's Iconic Department Store

El Corte Inglés isn't just a department store—it's a Spanish institution. Whether you're looking for high-end fashion, gourmet food, cutting-edge electronics, or everyday essentials, this store has everything under one roof. With locations in every major city across Spain, it's a go-to shopping destination for both locals and tourists.

In this guide, we will take you through the history, top departments, best locations, and must-visit services that make **El Corte Inglés** an unforgettable shopping experience.

A Brief History of El Corte Inglés

El Corte Inglés started as a **small tailor shop in Madrid in 1890**. Over the years, it grew into **Spain's largest department store chain** and one of the most recognized brands in Europe. Today, it operates in **over 90 locations across Spain and Portugal**, offering everything from **luxury brands to Spanish delicacies**.

Why Shop at El Corte Inglés?

✔ **All-in-One Shopping** – From **fashion to electronics, beauty products to gourmet food**, you'll find everything in one place.

✔ **High-Quality Brands** – It stocks both **international luxury brands** and **affordable Spanish labels**.

✔ **Tourist Services** – Special tax-free shopping, multilingual staff, and concierge services make it **tourist-friendly**.

✔ **Authentic Spanish Products** – The **gourmet food section** is perfect for bringing home a taste of Spain.

Top Departments & What to Buy

1. Fashion & Accessories

El Corte Inglés is famous for its **wide range of clothing and accessories**, featuring brands like:

- **Luxury Fashion:** Gucci, Prada, Balenciaga, Louis Vuitton.

- **Spanish Designers:** Adolfo Domínguez, Roberto Verino, Pedro del Hierro.

- **Affordable Fashion:** Zara, Mango, Massimo Dutti, Stradivarius.

- **Accessories & Watches:** Rolex, Cartier, Tous, Bimba y Lola.

📍 **Where to Find It?**

- **Madrid:** El Corte Inglés Castellana (*Best for luxury shopping*).
- **Barcelona:** El Corte Inglés Plaça Catalunya (*Great for designer & high-street brands*).

2. Gourmet Food & Spanish Delicacies

One of the best things about El Corte Inglés is its **gourmet supermarket**, offering:

- Jamón Ibérico (Iberian ham).
- Spanish olive oils.
- Artisan cheeses (*Manchego, Idiazabal, Mahón*).
- Fine wines & cava.
- Traditional sweets like turrón & polvorones.

📍 **Best Store for Gourmet Shopping:**

- **El Corte Inglés Castellana (Madrid)** – *Largest selection of Spanish delicacies.*

3. Electronics & Home Appliances

Looking for the latest **Apple iPhone, Samsung gadgets, or top-tier home appliances**? El Corte Inglés has a **massive electronics section**, selling:

- **Laptops & Smartphones** – Apple, Samsung, HP, Lenovo.
- **Kitchen Appliances** – Thermomix, SMEG, Bosch.
- **TVs & Sound Systems** – Sony, LG, Bose.

📍 **Best Store for Electronics:**

El Corte Inglés Callao (Madrid) – *Huge selection of tech gadgets.*

4. Beauty & Cosmetics

If you love **luxury skincare, high-end perfumes, and premium beauty brands**, El Corte Inglés is the place to be. Top brands include:

- **Perfumes:** Chanel, Dior, Tom Ford, Carolina Herrera.
- **Skincare:** Estée Lauder, Lancôme, La Mer, Kiehl's.
- **Makeup:** MAC, NARS, Bobbi Brown, Charlotte Tilbury.

📍 **Best Store for Beauty Shopping:**

- **El Corte Inglés Serrano (Madrid)** – *Premium beauty section with VIP service.*

Best El Corte Inglés Locations in Spain

1. Madrid – El Corte Inglés Castellana *(Flagship Store)*

- 📍 **Address:** Calle de Raimundo Fernández Villaverde, 65, Tetuán, 28003 Madrid, Spain.

- 📞 **Phone:** +34 914 18 88 00.

- 🌐 **Website:** www.elcorteingles.es

- **Opening Hours**: Monday to Saturday, 10:00 AM – 10:00 PM; Sunday, 11:00 AM – 9:00 PM.

2. Barcelona – El Corte Inglés Plaça Catalunya

- 📍 **Address:** Avenida Diagonal, 617, 08028 Barcelona, Spain.
- 📞 **Phone:** +34 932 81 50 11.
- **Website**: www.elcorteingles.es
- **Opening Hours**: Monday to Saturday, 9:00 AM – 9:00 PM.

3. Málaga – El Corte Inglés Avenida de Andalucía

- 📍 **Address:** Avenida de Andalucía, 4, 29007 Málaga, Spain.
- 📞 **Phone:** +34 952 07 65 00.
- **Website**: www.elcorteingles.es

- **Opening Hours**: Monday to Saturday, 10:00 AM – 10:00 PM; Closed Sundays.

Tourist Perks & Services

If you're visiting Spain, El Corte Inglés offers **special services** just for tourists:

✔ **Tax-Free Shopping** – If you're a non-EU resident, you can get up to **21% VAT refund** on your purchases.
✔ **Personal Shopper Service** – Get a **customized shopping experience** with expert fashion advice.
✔ **Home Delivery & Shipping** – They offer **international shipping** if you don't want to carry heavy bags.
✔ **Luxury Lounge** – Some locations have an **exclusive VIP lounge** for high-end shoppers.

📍 **Tourist Services Available At:**

- El Corte Inglés Castellana (Madrid).
- El Corte Inglés Plaça Catalunya (Barcelona).

Dining at El Corte Inglés: Best Places to Eat

Most major locations have **rooftop restaurants and gourmet food halls** where you can enjoy **Spanish cuisine with stunning city views**.

Best El Corte Inglés Restaurants

📍 **Gourmet Experience Callao (Madrid)** – *Panoramic views & tapas bar.*

📍 **Gourmet Experience Plaza Cataluña (Barcelona)** – *Fine dining with a view.*

El Corte Inglés isn't just a department store—it's part of Spain's culture. Whether you're shopping for fashion, indulging in gourmet food, or upgrading your gadgets, you'll find high-quality products and exceptional service. Plus, with tax-free shopping and premium customer services, it's one of the best places to shop in Spain.

Malaga's Best Shopping Streets and Malls

Málaga is more than just a beautiful coastal city—it's also a **shopper's paradise**. Whether you're looking for **luxury brands, unique local boutiques, traditional crafts, or bargain finds**, the city has something for everyone. From **bustling shopping streets to modern malls**, Málaga offers **a mix of old and new** that makes shopping an unforgettable experience.

In this guide, we will walk you through **the best shopping streets, top malls, and must-visit markets** in Málaga. Plus, **detailed contact information, addresses, and emails** for each place will be included to make your shopping trip as smooth as possible.

Best Shopping Streets in Málaga

If you prefer **open-air shopping** while enjoying the charm of Málaga's streets, head to these top locations:

1. Calle Larios – The Heart of Shopping in Málaga

Calle Marqués de Larios, or simply **Calle Larios**, is the most famous shopping street in Málaga. This elegant, pedestrian-only street is lined with **high-end brands, trendy boutiques, and stylish cafés**.

🛍️ **What to Buy:**

✔ **Luxury fashion:** Zara, Massimo Dutti, Mango.

✔ **Jewelry & accessories:** Pandora, Tous, Bimba y Lola.

✔ **Perfumes & cosmetics:** Sephora, Rituals, Kiko Milano.

📍 **Address:** Avenue de la Aurora, 25, Distrito Centro, 29002 Málaga, Spain.

📞 **Phone:** +34 952 36 93 93.

✉ **Website:** https://www.larioscentro.com/ES

- **Opening Hours**: Monday to Saturday, 10:00 AM – 12:00 AM.

2. Calle Nueva – Affordable Shopping & Local Boutiques

Just a few steps from Calle Larios, **Calle Nueva** offers a more **budget-friendly** shopping experience with **local fashion stores, accessories, and souvenirs**.

🛍️ **What to Buy:**

✔ Trendy fashion at lower prices.

✔ Handmade accessories and leather goods.

✔ Spanish shoes and handbags.

- 📍 **Address:** Calle Nueva, Distrito Centro, 29005 Málaga, Spain.

- ⏲ **Opening Hours**: Monday to Saturday, 10:00 AM – 8:00 PM.

3. Calle Especería & Calle San Juan – Hidden Shopping Gems

For a more **authentic and local shopping experience**, visit **Calle Especería and Calle San Juan**. These smaller streets are home to **family-run stores, artisan shops, and unique finds**.

🛍 **What to Buy:**

✔ Handmade leather goods.
✔ Traditional Andalusian ceramics.
✔ Locally made perfumes & soaps.

📍 **Address:** Calle Especería & Calle San Juan, 29005 Málaga, Spain.

⏲ **Opening Hours**: Monday to Saturday, 10:00 AM – 8:00 PM.

Best Shopping Malls in Málaga

If you prefer a **modern shopping experience** with air-conditioned comfort, Málaga's malls offer **a mix of international brands, dining, and entertainment**.

1. Muelle Uno – Shopping by the Sea

Muelle Uno is **a stylish open-air shopping center** located right by Málaga's harbor. It's a great spot for **boutique shopping, waterfront dining, and enjoying the sunset**.

🛍 **What to Buy:**

✔ **Designer clothes & accessories**

✔ **Handcrafted jewelry.**

✔ **Home decor & gifts.**

📍 **Address:** Paseo del Muello Uno, 4, 29016 Málaga, Spain.

📞 **Phone:** +34 952 00 39 42.

🌐 **Website:** www.muelleuno.com

🕐 **Opening Hours**: **Shops**: Daily, 10:00 AM – 12:00 AM, **Restaurants & Cafés**: Daily, 12:00 PM – Late.

2. Larios Centro – Popular Shopping Mall in the City Center

Larios Centro is one of the **most visited shopping malls in Málaga**, offering a mix of **fashion, electronics, and home goods**.

🛍 **What to Buy:**

✔ **Affordable fashion brands** – Primark, H&M, Stradivarius.

✔ **Electronics & gadgets** – MediaMarkt, Apple Store.

✔ **Home goods & decor** – Zara Home, Casa.

📍 **Address:** Avenida de la Aurora, 25, 29002 Málaga, Spain.

📞 **Phone:** +34 952 36 93 93.

🌐 **Website:** www.larioscentro.com

🕐 **Opening Hours**: Monday to Saturday, 10:00 AM – 12:00 AM, Closed on Sundays (except during special sales periods or holidays).

3. Plaza Mayor – The Best Outlet Shopping in Málaga

If you love **discount shopping**, head to **Plaza Mayor**, Málaga's **largest outlet mall** with **big-brand discounts**. It's located near the airport and is **worth the trip** for bargain hunters.

🛍 **What to Buy:**

✔ **Discounted luxury brands** – Nike, Adidas, Polo Ralph Lauren.

✔ **Spanish fashion brands** – Desigual, Mango Outlet.

✔ **Accessories & perfumes** – Sunglass Hut, The Body Shop.

📍 **Address:** Calle Alfonso Ponce de León, 3, 29004 Málaga, Spain.

📞 **Phone:** +34 952 24 75 80.

🌐 **Website:** www.plazamayor.es

🕐 **Opening Hours**: Daily, 10:00 AM – 10:00 PM.

Best Markets in Málaga for Local Crafts & Souvenirs

If you're looking for **authentic souvenirs, handmade goods, and fresh produce**, Málaga's local markets are **a must-visit**.

1. Mercado Central de Atarazanas – Traditional Market

Atarazanas Market is Málaga's **most famous food market**, filled with **fresh seafood, fruits, cheeses, and spices**.

🛍 **What to Buy:**

✔ Local olives & olive oil.
✔ Traditional Spanish cheeses.
✔ Fresh seafood & local delicacies.

📍 **Address:** Calle Atarazanas, 10, 29005 Málaga, Spain.

2. Mercado de la Merced – Artisan Market & Food Hall

A smaller but trendy market, **Mercado de la Merced** combines **local crafts, street food, and gourmet stalls**.

🛍 **What to Buy:**

✔ Handmade souvenirs & ceramics.

208 | MALAGA TRAVEL GUIDE 2025

✔ Artisan cheeses & wines.

✔ Authentic Andalusian spices.

📍 **Address:** Calle Merced, 4, 29012 Málaga, Spain.

Málaga has something for every shopper. Whether you prefer **luxury brands on Calle Larios, bargain hunting at Plaza Mayor, or finding unique souvenirs in local markets**, this city **won't disappoint**.

My advice? Start with **Calle Larios and Muelle Uno** for fashion, then visit **Plaza Mayor for outlet deals**, and finally, check out **Mercado de Atarazanas for traditional Spanish goods**.

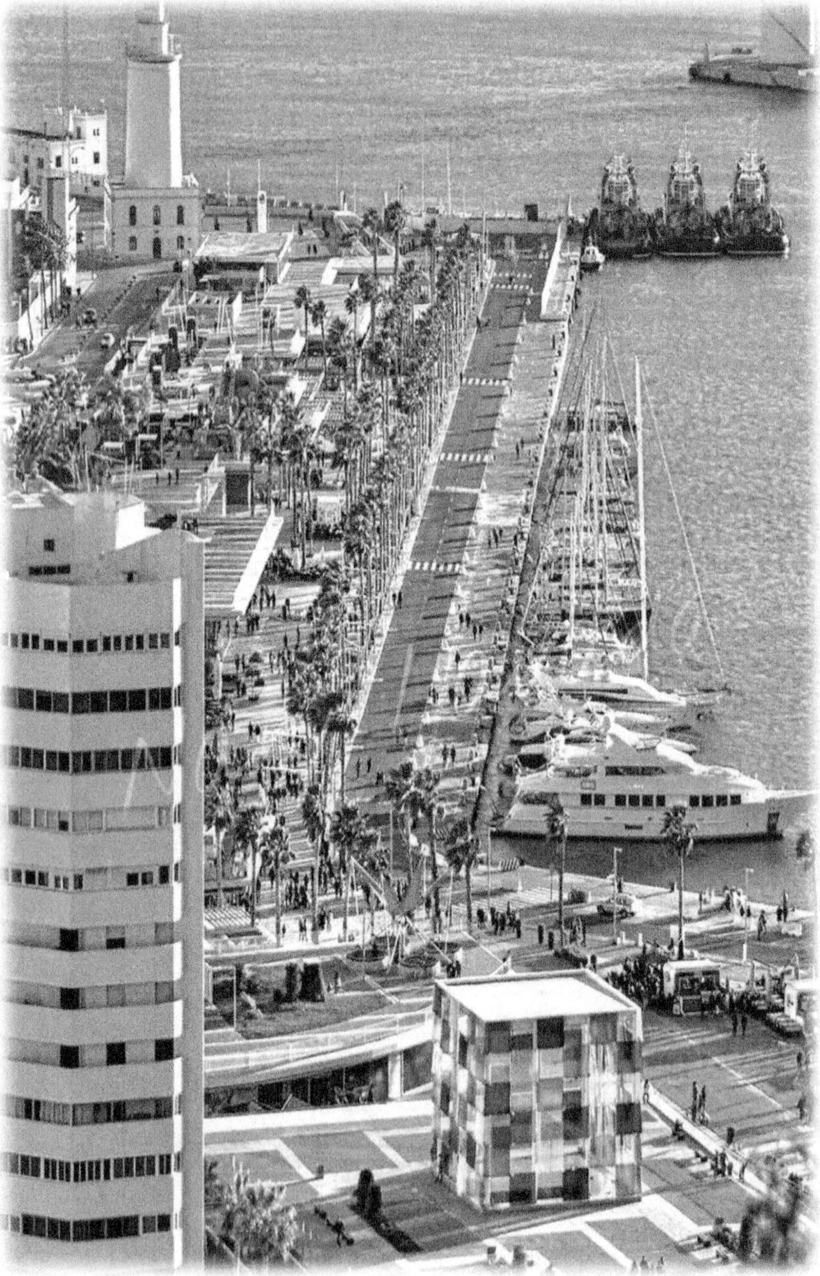

Chapter 8

Exploring Andalusia – Mountains, Beaches and Cultural Treasures

Andalusia is a region of contrasts, offering everything from majestic mountain towns and ancient cities to sun-kissed beaches and thrilling natural adventures. In this chapter, we'll uncover some of Andalusia's most unforgettable destinations, including the stunning mountaintop town of **Ronda** and the coastal beauty of **Nerja**, we'll also delve into **Granada's iconic Alhambra** and take you on a daring journey along **the Caminito del Rey**, a pathway suspended above breathtaking gorge

211 | MALAGA TRAVEL GUIDE 2025

Ronda: A Majestic Mountain Town

Ronda, perched dramatically on the cliffs of **El Tajo Gorge**, is one of Andalusia's most breathtaking destinations. Its rich history, natural beauty, and cultural significance make it a must-visit for anyone exploring southern Spain. Whether you're marveling at its iconic bridges, savoring local cuisine, or discovering its deep ties to **bullfighting traditions**, Ronda promises an unforgettable journey.

Getting to Ronda

Ronda is well-connected to Málaga, Seville, and other parts of Andalusia, making it easily accessible by car, train, or bus.

🚙 **By Car**: Driving to Ronda offers some of the most scenic views in Andalusia. From Málaga, take the **A-357 and A-367 roads**, which take about **1 hour 45 minutes**. If traveling from Marbella, the **A-397 mountain road** provides stunning panoramas.

🚆 **By Train**: The **RENFE train service** connects Ronda with Málaga, Seville, and Madrid. The journey from Málaga takes around **2 hours**, offering a relaxing and picturesque ride.

📍 **Ronda Train Station**

Address: Calle Victoria, 31, 29012 Ronda, Málaga, Spain.

📞 **Phone:** +34 912 320 320.

🌐 **Website:** www.renfe.com

🚌 **By Bus**: Direct buses from Málaga, Marbella, and Seville offer a budget-friendly option.

📍 **Ronda Bus Station**

Address: Calle de José María Castelló Madrid, 3, 29400 Ronda, Málaga, Spain.

📞 **Phone:** +34 952 87 22 62.

Top Attractions in Ronda

1. Puente Nuevo – The Iconic Bridge

The **Puente Nuevo**, Ronda's most recognizable symbol, spans the **El Tajo Gorge** at a height of **120 meters**. Built in 1793, it connects the old Moorish quarter with the newer parts of the town. The views from the bridge and surrounding viewpoints are simply breathtaking.

- **Address:** Puente Nuevo, 29400 Ronda, Spain.

- **Phone:** +34 649 96 53 38.

- **Website:** https://www.turismoderonda.es/

- **Tip:** Visit at **sunset** for the best views and photos!

2. Plaza de Toros – The Birthplace of Modern Bullfighting

One of Spain's oldest bullrings, the **Plaza de Toros de Ronda**, dates back to 1785. Known as the birthplace of modern bullfighting, the bullring features a **museum** detailing the history and traditions of the practice.

- **Address:** Paseo Reding, 20, Málaga-Este, 29016 Málaga, Spain.

🌐 **Website:** https://plazadetoroslamalagueta.com/

🎫 **Entrance Fee:** €8 (includes museum access).

3. The Old Town – A Walk Through History

Ronda's old town, known as **La Ciudad**, is filled with **cobbled streets, historic churches, and hidden squares**. Some must-visit spots include:

- **Palacio de Mondragón** (Ronda's small but charming history museum)

- **Casa del Rey Moro** (A house with a secret water mine)

- **Arab Baths** (Well-preserved medieval Moorish baths)

📍 **Address:** 5, Callle Santos, Malaga Centro, Malaga.

4. Alameda del Tajo – The Best Viewpoint in Ronda

This public park offers some of the **best panoramic views** of the surrounding countryside and mountains. Stroll through its shaded paths and enjoy the peaceful atmosphere, making it a perfect spot for relaxation or a picnic.

📍 **Address:** Calle Virgen de la Paz, 29400 Ronda, Málaga, Spain.

🕐 **Opening Hours:** Daily, 9:00 AM – 10:00 PM.

Where to Eat in Ronda

1. Restaurante Pedro Romero – Best for Traditional Andalusian Cuisine

A classic Ronda restaurant **opposite the bullring**, serving **bull tail stew, Iberian ham, and local wines**.

- **Address:** Calle Virgen de la Paz, 18, 29400 Ronda, Spain.
- **Phone:** +34 952 87 11 10.
- **Website:** https://www.rpedroromero.com/

2. Bodega San Francisco – Best for Tapas

A casual spot in **Plaza Ruedo Alameda**, serving **authentic tapas and local wine**.

- **Address:** Pje. del Cante, 1, 29400 Ronda, Málaga, Spain.
- **Phone:** +34 952 87 81 62.

3. Casa María – A Hidden Gem

A **family-run restaurant** where there's **no menu**—they simply bring out **the best seasonal dishes**!

📍 **Address:** Avenue de José Ortega y Gasset, 491, Campanillas, 29004 Málaga, Spain.

📞 **Phone:** +34 952 34 60 47.

🕐 **Opening Hours**: Monday to Saturday, 8:00 AM – 6:00 PM, Closed on Sundays.

Where to Stay in Ronda

Luxury Stay: Parador de Ronda

A stunning **4-star hotel** with rooms overlooking **El Tajo Gorge**.

📍 **Address:** Plaza de España, 29400 Ronda, Spain.

📞 **Phone:** +34 952 87 75 00.

🌐 **Website:** www.parador.es

Mid-Range: Hotel Montelirio

A great hotel in **a 17th-century palace**, offering **gorgeous river views**.

📍 **Address:** Calle Tenorio, 8, 29400 Ronda, Spain.

📞 **Phone:** +34 952 87 38 55.

🌐 **Website:** www.hotelmontelirio.com

Budget-Friendly: Hotel Andalucía

Hotel Andalucía is located near Ronda's train station, making it a convenient base for travelers arriving by rail.

📍 **Address:** Avenida Martínez Astein, 19, 29400 Ronda, Spain.

📞 **Phone:** +34 952 87 54 50.

🌐 **Website:** https://www.hotel-andalucia.net/es/

Day Trips from Ronda

- **Setenil de las Bodegas** – A unique white village with **houses built into cliffs**. (25 minutes by car).

- **Grazalema** – A stunning **natural park and mountain village**, perfect for hiking. (30 minutes by car).

- **Júzcar** – Known as the **"Smurf Village"** because of its **blue-painted houses**. (35 minutes by car).

Ronda is **a magical destination** that blends **history, nature, and Andalusian charm**. Whether you're crossing **Puente Nuevo**, sipping wine in the old town, or admiring sunset views, Ronda will **leave you speechless**.

💡 **My Advice?** Stay at least **one night** to fully enjoy the atmosphere. And don't forget your camera—this town is one of the most photogenic places in Spain! 📷 ✨

Nerja: Beaches, Caves, and Picturesque Views

Nerja is a **coastal paradise** on Spain's Costa del Sol, known for its **stunning beaches, breathtaking viewpoints, and the famous Nerja Caves**. It's the perfect escape if you love **sunshine, natural beauty, and a laid-back Andalusian atmosphere**.

Whether you're strolling through the **Balcony of Europe**, exploring the **mystical caves**, or relaxing on **crystal-clear beaches, Nerja has something for everyone**. This guide will take you through the **best things to do in Nerja**, where to eat, where to stay, and how to make the most of your trip. All the practical details, including addresses, contact information, and tips, are included to help you plan your visit seamlessly.

How to Get to Nerja

🚐 **By Car**: The best way to reach Nerja is by car. From Málaga, take the **A-7 highway (Autovía del Mediterráneo)**, and you'll arrive in **less than an hour**. The roads are scenic, passing through **coastal cliffs and rolling hills**.

- 🚍 **By Bus**: Regular buses run from Málaga to Nerja, operated by **ALSA**. The journey takes about **1 hour** and is an affordable option.

- 🚇 **By Train**: There is **no direct train to Nerja**. The closest train station is **Málaga María Zambrano**, from where you'll need to take a bus.

Nerja Bus Station

- **Address:** Av. Pescia, 29780 Nerja, Spain.
- **Phone:** +34 902 422 242.
- **Website:** www.alsa.es

Top Attractions in Nerja

1. Balcón de Europa – The Best View in Nerja

The **Balcón de Europa (Balcony of Europe)** is Nerja's most famous **viewpoint**, offering **panoramic sea views**. It's a **beautiful promenade** lined with **palm trees, benches, and street performers**.

- **Address:** Plaza Balcón de Europa, 29780 Nerja, Spain.
- **Tip:** Visit at **sunset** for the most stunning views! 📷

2. Nerja Caves – A Hidden Underground World

One of **Spain's most spectacular caves**, the **Cueva de Nerja** stretches over **5 kilometers** and features **massive rock formations, prehistoric cave paintings, and the world's largest stalactite**.

- **Address:** Carretera de Maro, s/n, 29787, Nerja, Spain.
- **Phone:** +34 952 52 95 20.
- **Website:** www.cuevadenerja.es
- **Opening Hours**: Daily, 9:30 AM – 3:30 PM.
- **Entrance Fee:** €13 for adults, €11 for seniors, €5 for children.

3. Playa de Burriana – The Best Beach in Nerja

This Blue Flag beach is perfect for sunbathing, swimming, and enjoying beachside restaurants. It has golden sand, clear waters, and plenty of water sports options.

- **Address:** Playa de Burriana, 29780 Nerja, Spain.
- **Facilities:** Sunbeds, showers, restaurants, parking.
- **Opening Hours**: Daily, at all hours.
- **Website:** https://www.nerja-turismo.com/

4. Playa de Maro – A Hidden Gem

If you're looking for **a quiet, natural beach**, this is the one! It's **surrounded by cliffs**, making it one of the most scenic spots in Nerja. **Snorkeling and kayaking** are popular here.

- **Address:** Playa de Maro, 29780 Nerja, Spain.
- **Opening Hours**: Daily, at all hours.

5. Frigiliana – The Most Beautiful White Village

Just a 15-minute drive from Nerja, **Frigiliana** is a picturesque white village filled with narrow cobblestone streets, colorful flower pots, and artisan shops.

- **Address:** Frigiliana, 29788 Málaga, Spain.
- **Phone:** +34 952 53 42 61.
- **Tip:** Wander through the **old Moorish quarter** for the most **Instagram-worthy** spots!

Where to Eat in Nerja

1. Restaurante Ayo – Best for Paella

A Nerja **legend**, Ayo is famous for its **giant paellas cooked over an open fire**. The best part? **You can ask for second helpings—for free!**

- **Address:** Playa de Burriana, 29780 Nerja, Spain.
- **Phone:** +34 952 52 22 89.
- **Opening Hours**: Daily, 12:00 AM – 6:00 PM.

- **Website:** https://ayonerja.com/

2. Oliva – A Modern Dining Experience

A stylish restaurant offering a blend of **modern Mediterranean dishes** with locally sourced ingredients.

- **Address:** Calle Pintada, 7, 29780 Nerja, Spain.
- **Phone:** +34 952 52 29 88.

- **Website:** www.restauranteoliva.com

Where to Stay in Nerja

Luxury Stay: Parador de Nerja

A **4-star hotel** on a cliff overlooking the sea, with **direct access to the beach via an elevator.**

- **Address:** Calle Almuñécar, 8, 29780 Nerja, Spain.
- **Phone:** +34 952 52 00 50.
- **Website:** www.parador.es

Mid-Range: Hotel Balcón de Europa

A comfortable **seafront hotel** located right next to the **Balcón de Europa**.

- **Address:** Paseo Balcón de Europa, 1, 29780 Nerja, Spain.
- **Phone:** +34 952 52 08 00.
- **Website:** www.hotelbalcondeeuropa.com

Budget Stay: Hostal Marissal

A budget-friendly guesthouse **right on the main square**, with simple but comfortable rooms.

- **Address:** Paseo Balcón de Europa, 3, 29780 Nerja, Malaga, Spain.
- **Phone:** +34 952 52 01 99.
- **Website**: www.hostalmarissal.com

Excursions & Activities

Kayak & Snorkeling Tour – Explore the coastline and discover hidden caves.

Contact: Educare Aventura

- **Address:** Camino de Burriana Local 2, Cam. de Burriana, 28, 29780 Nerja, Málaga, Spain.

- 📞 +34 952 03 90 26. 🌐 www.educare-aventura.com
- 💰 **Price Range**: Approximately €25 to €45.

Boat Trips – Take a cruise along the Costa del Sol.
Contact: Maro Adventures

- 📞 +34 652 78 19 34. 🌐 www.maroadventures.com
- 💶 **Price Range**: Approximately €50 - €150 per person.

Hiking in the Río Chíllar – Walk through a scenic river trail surrounded by waterfalls.

- 📍 **Start Point:** Calle Puente Viejo, 29780 Nerja, Spain.

Nerja is **one of the most beautiful towns on the Costa del Sol**, offering a **perfect mix of beach life, history, and adventure**. Whether you're here for **a short visit or an extended stay**, you'll fall in love with its **charming streets, relaxed vibe, and incredible views**.

💡 **My Advice?** Don't rush through Nerja—**take your time, soak in the beauty, and enjoy every moment!** 🌊 ✨

Granada and the Alhambra: A Must-See Day Trip

Granada, nestled at the foot of the Sierra Nevada mountains, is one of Spain's most historic cities. Known for its Moorish heritage, rich culture, and iconic monuments, Granada offers an unforgettable journey through time. The city's crown jewel, the **Alhambra**, is a UNESCO World Heritage Site and one of the most visited landmarks in Spain. From exploring the palaces of the Nasrid dynasty to enjoying tapas in lively plazas, Granada promises a unique experience.

Let's dive into how to make the most of a **day trip to Granada** and explore all it has to offer.

How to Get to Granada

By Car

Driving to Granada is scenic and straightforward. From Málaga, the drive takes around 1 hour 30 minutes via the **A-92 highway**.

By Train

RENFE operates regular high-speed trains (AVE) to Granada from Madrid, Málaga, and Seville. The train from Madrid takes approximately 3 hours and 30 minutes.

By Bus

If you don't have a car, you can catch a bus from **Málaga** or other nearby cities to Granada. The **bus ride takes around 2 hours**.

📍 Granada Bus Station

- **Address:** Avenida de Juan Pablo II, 18014 Granada, Spain.
- **Phone:** +34 902 42 22 42.
- **Website:** https://www.andalucia.org/es/inicio

📍 Granada Train Station

- **Address:** Avda. de Andaluces, 18014 Granada, Spain.
- **Website:** www.renfe.com

Top Attractions in Granada

1. The Alhambra – Granada's Iconic Palace Complex

The Alhambra is a magnificent complex of **palaces, gardens, and fortresses** that showcase the artistic and architectural brilliance of the **Nasrid dynasty**. Highlights include the **Palacios Nazaríes (Nasrid Palaces)** with their intricate tilework and arches, the **Generalife Gardens** known for their serene beauty, and the **Alcazaba**, a fortress with panoramic views of the city.

📍 Alhambra Palace

- **Address:** Calle Real de la Alhambra, s/n, 18009 Granada, Spain.
- 📞 **Phone:** +34 958 02 79 71.
- 🎫 **Entrance Fee**: Starting at €14 (prices vary depending on the time of year and the areas you wish to visit). It's highly recommended to **book tickets in advance**, as they sell out fast!
- 🌐 **Website:** www.alhambra-patronato.es
- 🕐 **Opening Hours**: Daily, 8:30 AM – 8:00 PM.
- 💡 **Tip: Arrive early** to beat the crowds and have more time to explore.

2. Mirador de San Nicolás: The Best View of the Alhambra

If you want that **iconic view** of the Alhambra with the Sierra Nevada mountains in the background, head to the **Mirador de San Nicolás**. It's the perfect spot to snap a photo and take in the **beauty of Granada**.

- **Address:** Plaza de San Nicolás, 18010 Granada, Spain.
- 🎫 **Entrance Fee**: Free entry.

- 🌐 **Website:** https://miradorsanicolas.com/
- 🕓 **Opening Hours**: Daily, at all hours.
- 💡 **Tip:** If you're here at sunset, the view is absolutely magical as the Alhambra is bathed in golden light.

3. Albaicín: A Neighborhood Steeped in History

The **Albaicín** is Granada's **old Muslim quarter**, with its narrow, winding streets, whitewashed houses, and **Arabian influence**. Walking through this neighborhood feels like stepping back in time.

You can explore the **Carmen de los Mártires**, a beautiful garden and palace, or just wander around and **get lost** in the **charming alleys**.

📍 **Address:** Albaicín, 18010 Granada, Spain.

4. Cathedral of Granada and Royal Chapel

The **Granada Cathedral**, a masterpiece of Renaissance and Baroque architecture, is a must-visit landmark. Adjacent to it, the **Royal Chapel** houses the tombs of **Queen Isabella I and**

King Ferdinand II, who sponsored Christopher Columbus' voyages.

- **Address:** Pl. de las Pasiegas, s/n, Centro, 18001 Granada.
- **Phone:** +34 958 22 29 59.
- **Entrance Fee**: €5 for the Cathedral, €5 for the Royal Chapel.
  Website: www.catedraldegranada.com
- **Opening Hours**: Monday to Saturday, 10:00 AM – 6:00 PM, Sundays, 3:00 PM – 6:30 PM.

Where to Eat in Granada

1. Bodegas Castañeda – Try the Local Vermut

A traditional **Granadian tavern** where you can enjoy **tapas with your drink**. It's a local favorite for its **vermut (sweet, aromatic wine)** and **classic Andalusian dishes**.

- **Address:** Almireceros, 1-3, 18010 Granada, Spain.
- **Phone:** +34 958 21 54 64.
- **Price Range**: Approximately €10 to €25 per person.
- **Opening Hours**: Daily, 11:30 AM – 12:30 AM.

2. Restaurante Ruta del Azafrán – Fusion Cuisine

Located at the foot of the Alhambra, this restaurant blends **Mediterranean and Arabic flavors** in a unique menu. Don't miss the **couscous with lamb**.

- **Address:** Paseo del Padre Manjón, 1, 18010 Granada, Spain.

- **Phone:** +34 958 22 68 82.

- **Website:** https://rutadelazafran.com/

- **Price Range:** Approximately €30 to €45 per person.
- **Opening Hours:** Daily, 1 PM – 11:00 PM.

Where to Stay in Granada

Luxury Stay: Parador de Granada

Located **inside the Alhambra complex**, the **Parador de Granada** is a **historic hotel** set in a **monastery**. You'll wake up with views of the **Alhambra** and enjoy a luxurious experience.

- **Address:** Alhambra, s/n, 18009 Granada, Spain.
- **Phone:** +34 958 22 14 40.
- **Website:** www.parador.es

Mid-Range: Hotel Casa 1800 Granada

A **boutique hotel** located near the **Albaicín**, with **charming rooms** and an excellent location for sightseeing.

- ⚲ **Address:** Calle Benalúa, 11, 18010 Granada, Spain.
- 📞 **Phone:** +34 958 21 07 00.
- 🌐 **Website:** www.hotelcasa1800granada.com

Budget Stay: Hostal Verónica

A **budget-friendly** option in the **city center**. It's a simple, no-frills hotel with clean rooms and a **great location** for exploring Granada on foot.

- ⚲ **Address:** Calle Ángel, 17, Centro, 18002 Granada, Spain.
- 📞 **Phone:** +34 958 22 66 23.
- 🌐 **Website:** https://www.hostalveronicacentro.com/

A **day trip to Granada** is **absolutely worth it**, especially for first-timers. The **Alhambra** is a once-in-a-lifetime experience, but the city itself has so much more to offer. The **stunning views**, **rich history**, and **vibrant local life** make Granada a **memorable and enriching** destination.

💡 **Pro Tip:** Granada is famous for its **free tapas** with a drink—so order a drink and enjoy a **complimentary tapa** while you explore the city! 🏰 🍷 .

The Caminito del Rey: An Adventure for Nature Lovers

If you're a nature lover with a **taste for adventure**, then **the Caminito del Rey** should be at the top of your list. Located in **the province of Málaga**, Spain, this iconic **mountain path** offers a unique blend of **stunning views, thrilling heights**, and an unforgettable experience. Known as **"The King's Little Path"**, this trail was once considered one of the **most dangerous paths** in the world, but today it's been carefully restored to allow visitors to safely experience its dramatic beauty.

So, let's talk about why **Caminito del Rey** is a must-do adventure and everything you need to know to make the most of your hike.

What is the Caminito del Rey?

The **Caminito del Rey** is a **3-kilometer path** that stretches along the **El Chorro Gorge**, which is nestled between the **mountain cliffs** in **the natural park of Desfiladero de los Gaitanes**. The trail is built into the sides of steep cliffs, with **narrow wooden walkways** hanging high above the river below. While the path once had a reputation for being perilous, it has been **completely renovated** and is now safe for hikers to enjoy, with secure handrails and well-maintained paths.

What makes this place so special is the **breathtaking views**, the **sense of adventure**, and the **intimate connection with nature** that you experience as you make your way across the gorge.

How to Get There

By Car

The drive from Málaga takes about **1 hour** via the **A-357 and MA-5403 roads**. Parking is available near the trailhead in **Ardales** or **El Chorro**.

By Train

You can take a **train** from Málaga to **El Chorro**, the nearest station to the Caminito del Rey. From there, it's a short **bus ride or walk** to the trail's entrance.

📍 El Chorro Train Station

- **Address:** Estación de El Chorro, 29552 Álora, Málaga, Spain.
- 📞 **Phone:** +34 912 320 320.
- 🌐 **Website:** www.renfe.com

By Bus

Buses operate from Málaga and other nearby towns to **El Chorro** or **Ardales**, providing a budget-friendly way to reach the Caminito. Be sure to **check schedules** in advance.

📍 El Chorro Bus Stop

• **Address**: Calle Conde del Guadalhorce, 29552 Álora, Málaga, Spain.

Tickets and Practical Information

🎟 **Entrance Fee**:
• Standard Ticket: €10.
• Guided Tour: €18.

⏰ **Opening Hours**:
• Tuesday to Sunday: 9:30 AM – 5:00 PM
• Closed on Mondays

How to Hike the Caminito del Rey

The **hike** itself is relatively short, but don't let the length fool you—it's a **thrilling** experience. The walk starts at the **north entrance**, where you'll be provided with safety instructions and a helmet. The **trail takes around 2-3 hours to complete**, depending on your pace.

What to Expect

- **Hiking Time:** 2-3 hours.
- **Distance:** 3 km (1.9 miles).
- **Elevation Gain:** 100 meters.

The Path

The trail is laid out with **well-maintained wooden planks**, and you'll find **handrails** to keep you steady as you walk along the cliffs. Along the way, you'll cross **several suspension bridges**, giving you **stunning views** of the gorge below.

What to Bring

- **Comfortable Shoes**: The path is relatively easy, but sturdy shoes are recommended, especially if you're hiking after rain.
- **Water and Snacks**: There are no services along the trail, so it's essential to bring your own water.
- **Sunscreen**: The sun can be strong, especially in the summer months.
- **Camera**: You won't want to miss snapping some pictures of the incredible views!

What to Wear

Dress for comfort. It can get warm, especially during the summer months, so wear **light, breathable clothes**. And don't forget a **hat** and **sunglasses**.

Tickets and Booking

Due to the popularity of the Caminito del Rey, it's essential to **book your tickets in advance**. You can purchase them online through the official **Caminito del Rey website**.

Ticket Information:

- **General Admission**: €10.

- **Guided Tour (Optional):** €18

It's also possible to purchase tickets **on-site**, but it's much safer to **book ahead** to avoid missing out, especially during high season.

📍 **Ticket Booking Website:** www.caminitodelrey.info

Where to Stay Nearby

After your thrilling adventure on the Caminito del Rey, you'll want to relax and enjoy the surrounding area. Here are a few **accommodation options**.

1. Luxury Stay: Complejo Turístico La Garganta

An elegant hotel offering **gorge views**, a pool, and a restaurant featuring Andalusian cuisine.

- 📍 **Address:** Barriada El Chorro, s/n, 29552 Álora, Málaga, Spain.
- 📞 **Phone:** +34 952 49 50 00.
- 🌐 **Website:** www.lagarganta.com

2. Budget-Friendly: Hostal El Cruce

A budget-friendly option with clean rooms and a convenient location near the bus stop in Ardales.

- 📍 **Address:** Avenida de Málaga, 10, 29550 Ardales, Málaga, Spain.
- 📞 **Phone:** +34 952 45 71 23.

If you love adventure and nature, **the Caminito del Rey is a must-do**. The combination of **thrilling heights**, **jaw-dropping views**, and the sense of accomplishment you'll feel after completing the hike make it a **memorable experience**.

Whether you're a **serious hiker** or just someone who loves to explore, this trail offers something special for everyone. Don't forget to **plan ahead**, bring your camera, and take your time soaking in the beauty of this amazing natural wonder.

Important Contacts

Caminito del Rey Visitors Reception Center

- **Phone:** +34 951 95 00 99.

- **Address:** W6J6+Q4, 29550 Gobantes, Málaga, Spain.

- **Opening Hours**: Daily, 8:00 AM – 2:30 PM.
- **Website:** https://www.caminitodelrey.info/es/

Make sure to check out the official website for **up-to-date information**, safety tips, and ticket availability!

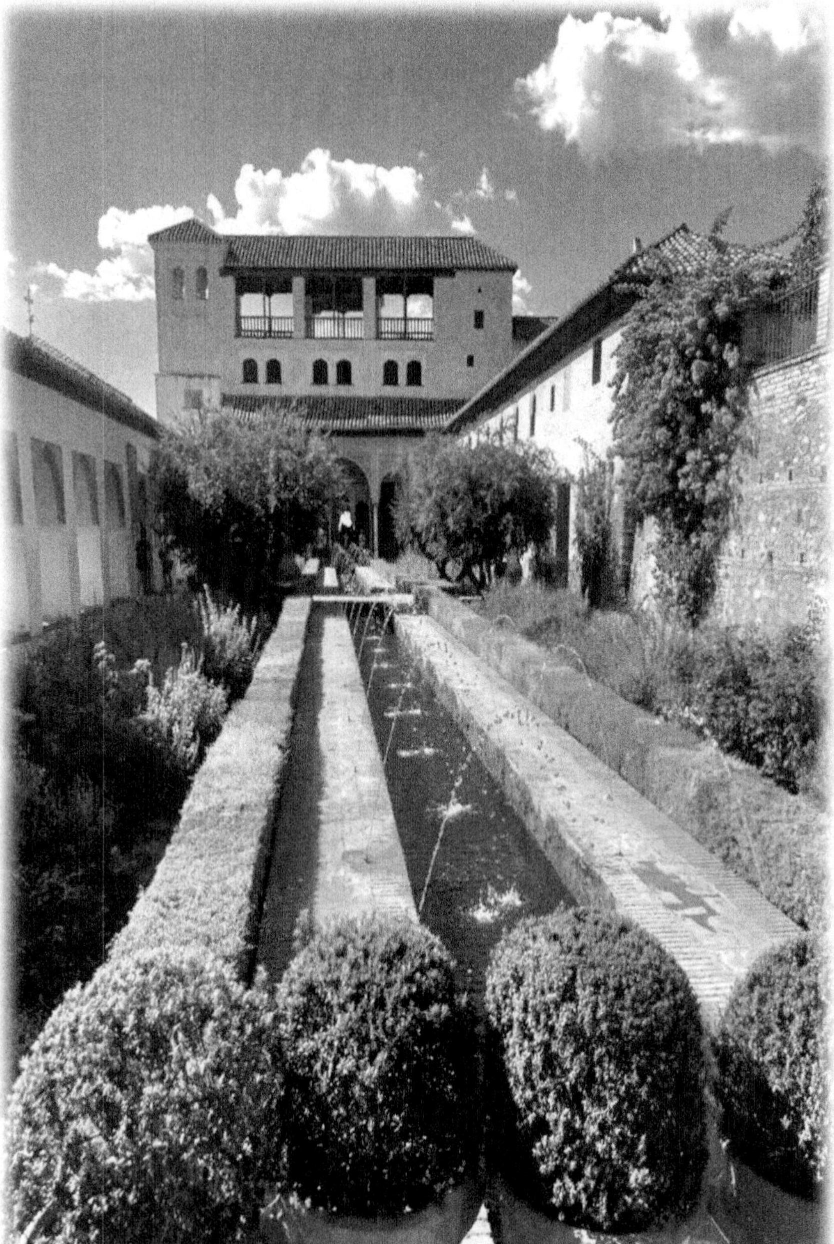

Chapter 9

Making the Most of Your Malaga Adventure

This chapter brings together everything you need to know to ensure your trip to Málaga is both memorable and seamless. From practical tips on budgeting, safety, and packing to navigating local customs and understanding cultural nuances, these insights will help you make the most of your visit. Whether it's your first time in Málaga or a return trip, this guide is designed to equip you with all the essential knowledge for a stress-free and enjoyable experience.

Budgeting for Your Trip: Tips for Affordable Travel

Traveling doesn't have to break the bank. With a little planning and smart choices, you can enjoy an amazing adventure without overspending. Whether you're heading to a **far-off destination** or exploring local treasures, budgeting is key to making the most of your trip without the financial stress. Here's how you can make your travel dreams a reality on a budget.

1. Plan Ahead for the Best Deals

One of the simplest ways to save money is to plan ahead. The earlier you book, the more likely you are to find **cheaper flights**, **accommodation**, and even **activities**. Don't wait until the last minute—by booking in advance, you can take advantage of early bird discounts and special offers.

How to do it:

- **Set up price alerts** on flight and hotel websites (e.g., **Skyscanner, Google Flights**).
- **Book flights** at least **two to three months in advance** for the best deals.

- Consider flying during off-peak seasons to save even more. Flights and accommodations are typically cheaper when fewer tourists are traveling.

2. Use Public Transportation

Transportation costs can add up quickly, especially if you're relying on taxis or rental cars. Save money by using **public transportation** wherever possible. Not only is it budget-friendly, but it also gives you a true sense of local life!

How to do it:

- **Research the local transportation options** before your trip. Many cities have **subways**, **buses**, and **trains** that are both affordable and efficient.
- **Buy multi-ride passes** or **weekly cards** if you'll be using public transport frequently.
- **Walk or bike** whenever possible—many cities are **walkable** and biking is a fun and **cost-effective** way to explore.

3. Choose Budget-Friendly Accommodation

Accommodation can take up a huge portion of your budget, but there are many ways to save without sacrificing comfort. From

hostels to **Airbnb** rentals, you have plenty of affordable options.

How to do it:

- **Look for hostels** if you're okay with sharing spaces. Many hostels offer private rooms for a fraction of the cost of hotels.

- **Check out Airbnb** for affordable, **local stays** that often offer better value and charm than traditional hotels.

- If you're traveling with a group, consider renting an entire apartment or house to split costs.

- **Stay outside tourist areas**. Accommodation in **city centers** or tourist hotspots tends to be pricier. Find a place a little farther out, but still close to public transport.

4. Eat Like a Local

Eating out in popular tourist spots can quickly drain your budget. Instead of dining in pricey restaurants, get to know where the locals go and enjoy more affordable meals.

How to do it:

- Eat at local markets or street food vendors. You'll find delicious meals at a fraction of the cost compared to touristy restaurants.

- Cook your own meals if you have access to a kitchen. Stock up on fresh ingredients from local markets and enjoy the experience of making your own meals.

- If you do go to a restaurant, try to avoid tourist menus and look for places where locals eat—they'll likely have better prices and tastier food.

5. Take Advantage of Free and Low-Cost Activities

You don't have to spend a fortune to enjoy great activities. Many cities and destinations offer **free attractions** or activities that are both fun and enriching.

How to do it:

- Look for **free walking tours**—many cities offer these as a great introduction to their history and culture.

- Visit **public parks**, **beaches**, and **museums** with **free entry** or **discounted rates**.

- Check out **local events** and **festivals** that are free or low-cost to attend. You can enjoy music, dancing, and other activities without spending much.

- If you're a nature enthusiast, go for **hikes** or **swim in the sea**—these activities are often **free** and provide unforgettable experiences.

6. Set a Daily Budget

Before you even leave, decide how much money you're comfortable spending each day. Setting a daily budget will help keep your spending in check and ensure you have enough for the whole trip.

How to do it:

- Estimate how much you'll need for each day, including meals, transport, and any activities.
- Use a **travel budget calculator** to help you get a rough estimate.
- Carry cash to avoid overspending on credit cards—this will help you stick to your budget.

7. Travel with Friends or Family

Traveling in a group is one of the best ways to split costs. From **shared accommodation** to **group discounts** on tours, traveling with friends or family can make your trip **more affordable**.

How to do it:

- **Plan group activities** where you can share the cost of things like **tours, car rentals**, and **meals**.

- Look for **group discounts** for things like museums, attractions, and even transportation.

- Sharing accommodations like **Airbnb** or a house rental can drastically cut down on your accommodation costs.

8. Use Travel Reward Programs

If you're a frequent traveler, make sure to take advantage of travel rewards programs to save money on flights, hotels, and even activities.

How to do it:

- Sign up for **frequent flyer programs** and use credit cards that offer **travel rewards points**.

- **Redeem points** or miles for **free flights** or **upgrades** to make your trip more affordable.

- Look for **discounted activities** or **free tours** available through reward programs or special offers.

9. Travel During Off-Peak Times

Traveling during **off-peak seasons** can save you a lot of money. Flights, hotels, and activities are typically much **cheaper** when fewer people are traveling.

How to do it:

- Research the **low season** for your destination—traveling in the **fall** or **spring** can save you money while still offering great weather.

- Avoid **major holidays** and school breaks, as these tend to be the **most expensive times to travel**.

10. Track Your Expenses

As you go, keep track of your spending. This will help you stay within budget and prevent any surprises.

How to do it:

- Use a **travel budget app** or a simple **spreadsheet** to keep track of daily expenses.

- If you go over budget one day, try to spend a little less the next.

Traveling on a budget is all about making **smart choices** and being **resourceful**. From booking early to eating like a local and choosing affordable accommodation, there are plenty of ways to enjoy an amazing trip without the stress of overspending. With these tips, you'll be able to have a **memorable** and **affordable** travel experience that will leave you with plenty of great memories and a few extra euros in your pocket.

Safety Tips: What to Know for a Safe and Enjoyable Trip

Traveling is exciting, but staying safe while doing it is just as important. Whether you're strolling through the streets of Malaga or heading out to explore Andalusia, there are some simple safety tips that will help make sure your trip is not only fun but also safe and stress-free. Here are some things to keep in mind as you travel through this beautiful region:

1. Stay Alert in Crowded Areas

Like any popular tourist destination, Malaga can get crowded, especially in places like **Calle Larios**, **Plaza de la Merced**, and the **Alcazaba**. Pickpockets are often attracted to large crowds, so always keep an eye on your belongings.

Tips:

- Use a **money belt** or **crossbody bag** to keep valuables close to you.

- If you carry a backpack, wear it on your front in crowded areas.

- Avoid leaving your phone or wallet unattended on tables or benches.

2. Watch Out for the Sun

Malaga is sunny almost year-round, and while that's great for enjoying the outdoors, it's important to take care in the heat. Overexposure to the sun can lead to sunburn, dehydration, or heatstroke.

Tips:

- Wear **sunscreen** with a high SPF.
- Always carry a **water bottle** and stay hydrated.
- Wear a **hat** or **sunglasses** to protect your face and eyes from the sun.
- Avoid being in the sun too long between **12 PM and 4 PM** when it's at its hottest.

3. Stay Safe on the Beach

Malaga's beaches, such as **Playa de la Malagueta** and **Playa del Palo**, are some of the most popular spots to visit. But when you're enjoying the beach, remember that safety is key.

Tips:

- Always swim **between the flags** or in areas designated as safe by lifeguards.
- Be cautious of **strong waves** and **underwater currents**.

- Don't leave valuables unattended on the beach. Always bring a secure waterproof bag.

4. Use Reputable Transport Services

Malaga's public transport is generally safe, but it's still important to choose reputable services when moving around the city or traveling further afield.

Tips:

- **Taxis**: Always make sure you're getting into a licensed taxi. You can recognize a legal taxi by the **taxi meter** and **official license number**.

- **Public Transport**: Buses and trains are safe, but make sure you check the schedule and route ahead of time.

- **Scooters and Bikes**: When using electric scooters or bikes, always check the **condition** of the vehicle before riding. Stick to bike lanes and be aware of traffic.

Taxi Contact Information:

- **Radio Taxi Malaga**
   - **Phone**: +57 6617724.
   - **Address**: Principal Malaga, Malaga, Santander.

5. Keep Your Documents Safe

It's always a good idea to carry a **photocopy** of your passport, **travel insurance** information, and **emergency contact numbers**. This can come in handy in case anything gets lost or stolen.

Tips:

- Leave **original documents** in a safe at your hotel.
- Keep a digital copy of important documents on your phone or in the cloud.
- Always know where your **hotel's contact information** is in case you need assistance.

6. Emergency Numbers in Spain

While Spain is generally a safe country to travel in, it's always good to be prepared. Here are the important emergency numbers to keep handy.

Emergency Numbers:

- **Police**: 112.
- **Ambulance**: 061 or 112.
- **Fire Department**: 080 or 112.

- **Tourist Information**: +34 91 578 78 10.

7. Be Mindful of Local Customs and Laws

Different countries have different customs and laws, so it's important to be aware of local rules when you're in Malaga. Being respectful of these laws helps ensure your trip goes smoothly.

Tips:

- **Drinking alcohol**: Drinking alcohol in public spaces like parks or beaches is often **prohibited** unless you're in designated areas.

- **Dress code**: While **Malaga is relaxed**, modest dress is appreciated when visiting religious sites, such as **churches** or **cathedrals**. Be sure to cover your shoulders and knees when entering.

- **Smoking**: Smoking is not allowed indoors in public places, and there are designated areas for smokers in outdoor spaces.

8. Avoid Scams and Tourist Traps

Like in any popular tourist spot, there are a few scams that might try to take advantage of tourists. Whether it's overly aggressive street vendors or people asking for donations, it's always best to be cautious.

Tips:

- Be careful if someone tries to sell you something on the street, especially if they are too persistent.

- If someone offers you something for "free" (like a bracelet), they might expect you to pay once it's on your wrist.

9. Protect Your Health

While Malaga's healthcare system is excellent, it's always better to stay healthy throughout your trip. Here are some health-related tips to keep in mind:

Tips:

- If you have any **pre-existing medical conditions**, bring along the necessary **medications**.

- **Travel insurance** is essential. It'll help cover any unexpected medical expenses while you're abroad.

- If you feel unwell, there are plenty of **pharmacies** around the city, and the **hospital** is always available in emergencies.

Pharmacy Contact Information:

Farmacia Caffarena 24 Horas

Farmacia Caffarena is a 24-hour pharmacy located in the heart of Málaga, providing round-the-clock pharmaceutical services to residents and visitors.

- **Address**: Alameda Principal, 2, 29005 Málaga, Spain.
- **Phone**: +34 952 21 28 58.
- **Opening Hours:** Open 24 hours, 7 days a week

Farmacia Reding

Located at the front of the bullring, Farmacia Reding offers extended hours, making it convenient for those seeking pharmaceutical services late into the evening.

- **Address**: Paseo de Reding, 31, 29016 Málaga, Spain.
- **Phone:** +34 665 11 37 14.
- **Opening Hours:** Daily: 9:00 AM – 12:00 AM

Hospital Contact Information:

Hospital Regional Universitario de Malaga

This is a major public hospital offering a wide range of medical specialties and services.

- **Address**: Calle Carlos Haya, s/n, 29010 Málaga, Spain.
- **Phone**: +34 952 29 00 00.
- **Opening Hours:** Emergency services are available 24/7.

Hospital Quirónsalud Málaga

A leading private hospital equipped with state-of-the-art facilities and a team of specialized medical professionals.

- **Address**: Avenue de Imperio Argentina, 1, 29004 Málaga, Spain.
- **Phone:** +34 951 94 00 00.
- **Opening Hours:** Emergency services are available 24/7; other departments may have varying hours.

10. Trust Your Instincts

Above all else, trust your instincts. If something doesn't feel right, or if a situation seems suspicious, don't hesitate to remove yourself from it. **Malaga** is a wonderful city with a rich culture and friendly locals, but being cautious will ensure that your trip remains enjoyable and safe.

Safety is a top priority when traveling, but with a little preparation, you can ensure your time in **Malaga** is memorable for all the right reasons.

Packing Tips: What to Bring for Every Season

Packing can sometimes feel like a chore, especially when you're unsure about what to bring for a trip to a destination with varying seasons like **Malaga**. From the warm, sunny days of summer to the cooler nights in the winter, packing right can make all the difference. Here's a guide on what to pack for every season so you can enjoy your trip to Malaga without any worries!

1. What to Pack for Spring

Spring in **Malaga** is mild and pleasant. Temperatures typically range from **15°C to 20°C (59°F to 68°F)**, which is perfect for sightseeing and exploring.

Essential Items:

- **Light Jacket or Sweater**: It can get cool in the mornings and evenings, so packing a light jacket is a good idea.
- **Comfortable Shoes**: You'll likely be walking a lot around the city, so comfortable shoes are a must.

- **Layered Clothing**: Since the weather can change throughout the day, layer your clothes. T-shirts or long-sleeve shirts work great under a sweater or light jacket.

- **Sunglasses**: Spring often brings a lot of sunshine, so a good pair of sunglasses will protect your eyes.

- **Umbrella**: While it's usually dry, occasional spring showers do happen, so it's always smart to have a small, portable umbrella.

2. What to Pack for Summer

Malaga summers can be hot! With temperatures reaching **30°C to 40°C (86°F to 104°F)**, it's essential to be prepared for the heat.

Essential Items:

- **Light, Breathable Clothing**: Pack loose, breathable clothing made from materials like cotton or linen. This will keep you cool during the day.

- **Sun Protection**: Don't forget your **sunscreen** with a high SPF, a **hat**, and **sunglasses** to protect your face and eyes from the intense sun.

- **Swimwear**: Malaga's beaches are perfect for swimming and sunbathing, so pack your swimsuit.

- **Comfortable Sandals or Flip-Flops**: These are perfect for walking around the beach and for casual strolls around the city.

- **Reusable Water Bottle**: Staying hydrated is key in the summer heat, so always carry a water bottle.

Local Shops for Summer Essentials:

El Corte Inglés (for clothing and accessories)

- ○ **Address**: Av. de Andalucía, 4, 29006 Málaga, Spain.

3. What to Pack for Autumn

Autumn in **Malaga** is a beautiful time to visit. The weather is cooler, and the crowds are thinner. Temperatures range from **15°C to 25°C (59°F to 77°F)**.

Essential Items:

- **Light Jacket or Coat**: Autumn nights can get chilly, so bring a jacket or light coat for the evenings.

- **Scarf or Shawl**: A light scarf is perfect for adding warmth during cooler days or evenings.

- **Closed-toe Shoes**: Comfortable shoes are important, but you might want to opt for closed-toe shoes now that it's a bit cooler.

- **Jeans or Long Pants**: It's time to switch to pants as temperatures start to drop, but you won't need anything too heavy.

- **Camera**: Autumn is a fantastic time for photography with the beautiful colors and mild weather.

4. What to Pack for Winter

Winters in **Malaga** are generally mild compared to northern Europe, but they can still get a bit chilly, especially in the evenings. Daytime temperatures usually stay around **10°C to 20°C (50°F to 68°F)**, but nights can dip to **5°C (41°F)** or lower.

Essential Items:

- **Warm Jacket**: A light to medium-weight jacket should be sufficient for winter. If you're sensitive to the cold, you may want a heavier coat for the evenings.

- **Layers**: The key to packing for winter is layering. Bring sweaters, long-sleeve shirts, and scarves to layer on top of each other as needed.

- **Comfortable Boots**: If you plan on walking a lot, comfortable winter boots with a good grip are a smart choice for those colder days.

- **Gloves and Hat**: While it doesn't snow in Malaga, it can get cold in the evenings, so bringing a light pair of gloves and a hat will keep you warm.

Where to Find Winter Gear:

Decathlon (for outdoor clothing and accessories).

- o **Address**: Camino de la Loma de San Julián, A-7 salida San Julián, Zona Guadalmar, 29004 Málaga, Spain
- o **Phone**: +34 952 17 70 20.
- o **Website**: https://www.decathlon.es/
- o **Opening Hours**: Monday to Saturday: 9:30 AM – 9:30 PM; Closed on Sundays.

5. General Packing Tips for All Seasons

No matter the season, there are a few things you should always pack for your trip to Malaga:

- **Travel Adapter**: Spain uses the **Type C and F** plugs, so make sure to bring an adapter if you're traveling from abroad.
- **Camera**: Malaga is full of beautiful sights. You'll want to capture memories of everything from the **Alcazaba** to **Plaza de la Merced**.

- **Daypack or Small Backpack**: A small bag is perfect for carrying essentials like sunscreen, water, and a camera while you're out exploring.

- **Personal Medications**: If you take any medications, be sure to pack them, as pharmacies may not carry everything you need.

6. Packing for Excursions and Day Trips

If you're planning day trips to places like **Ronda** or **Nerja**, pack accordingly. Here's what you might need:

- **Comfortable Hiking Shoes**: If you're exploring **Caminito del Rey** or **Nerja caves**, sturdy shoes are essential.

- **Snacks and Water**: On longer day trips, it's a good idea to bring along snacks and water, especially for places where there are fewer shops.

- **Sunglasses and Sunscreen**: Even in winter, the sun can be strong, so make sure to protect your skin and eyes.

Packing for Malaga can be easy as long as you're prepared for the season you're visiting. From sunny beaches in the summer to cooler evenings in the winter, a little planning ahead will ensure that you have everything you need for a smooth and enjoyable trip. Whether you're strolling along **Calle Larios** or hiking through the beautiful **Sierra de las Nieves**, you'll be ready for whatever this stunning city has to offer.

Language and Cultural Etiquette in Malaga

When visiting Malaga, understanding some basic aspects of the local language and cultural etiquette can enhance your experience and make interactions smoother. While most people in the city can communicate in English, especially in tourist areas, it's always appreciated when visitors make an effort to speak the local language, Spanish. Here are some helpful tips for navigating language and cultural norms in Malaga:

1. Basic Spanish Phrases

Learning a few key phrases in Spanish can go a long way in making a positive impression. Here are some simple phrases that will help you get by:

Greetings and Introductions:

These common phrases are perfect for starting conversations and introducing yourself.

- **Hola** (Hello).
- **Buenos días** – Good morning.
- **Buenas tardes** – Good afternoon.
- **Buenas noches** – Good evening/night.

- **¿Cómo estás?** – How are you?
- **Me llamo [Your Name]** – My name is [Your Name].
- **¿Cómo te llamas?** – What is your name?
- **Encantado/a de conocerte** – Nice to meet you
- **Adiós** – Goodbye.
- **Hasta luego** – See you later.

Asking for Help or Information

These phrases are useful when you need assistance or directions.

- **¿Dónde está el baño?** – Where is the bathroom?
- **¿Cómo llego a [location]?** – How do I get to [location]?
- **¿Puede ayudarme?** – Can you help me?
- **No entiendo** – I don't understand.
- **¿Habla inglés?** – Do you speak English?
- **Necesito ayuda** – I need help.
- **¿Cuánto cuesta esto?** – How much does this cost?

Dining and Ordering Food

Use these phrases to enjoy meals at restaurants or order from local cafes.

- **Una mesa para [número], por favor** – A table for [number], please.

- **¿Me trae el menú, por favor?** – Can you bring me the menu, please?

- **Quisiera [dish/drink], por favor** – I would like [dish/drink], please.

- **¿Tiene opciones vegetarianas?** – Do you have vegetarian options?

- **La cuenta, por favor** – The bill, please.

- **Está delicioso** – It's delicious.

- **¿Qué recomienda?** – What do you recommend?

Shopping and Markets

Essential phrases for navigating stores and street markets.

- **¿Cuánto vale?** – How much is it?

- **¿Puedo probarlo?** – Can I try it?

- **¿Tiene este en otro color/talla?** – Do you have this in another color/size?

- **Solo estoy mirando, gracias** – I'm just looking, thank you

- **¿Aceptan tarjetas de crédito?** – Do you accept credit cards?

- **¿Me puede dar un descuento?** – Can you give me a discount?

Even if you don't speak Spanish fluently, locals appreciate the effort and will often switch to English to help you out if needed.

2. Cultural Etiquette and Norms

While Malaga is a welcoming and relaxed city, there are a few cultural etiquettes to keep in mind to ensure you're respectful to locals:

Greetings: In Spain, it's common to greet people with a kiss on each cheek, especially among friends and acquaintances. For formal or professional settings, a handshake is more common. When meeting someone, make sure to smile and make eye contact as a sign of respect.

Dining Etiquette: Spanish dining habits are a bit different from those in other countries, and understanding them will help you feel more at ease:

Meal Times: Spaniards eat later than many other countries. **Lunch** is typically around **2:00 PM to 3:00 PM**, and **dinner** doesn't usually begin until **9:00 PM to 10:00 PM**. Be mindful of these times when planning your meals.

Sharing Dishes: Tapas culture is all about sharing! If you're dining with friends or family, it's customary to order several dishes and share them. Don't hesitate to try a little of everything.

Personal Space: Spaniards tend to stand closer to each other while speaking, and conversations are often lively and animated. Don't be surprised if there's less personal space in crowded places—this is normal in many Mediterranean cultures.

Dress Code: Malaga, like much of Spain, has a relatively relaxed dress code, especially in warmer months. However, in more upscale places or restaurants, people tend to dress smart-casual. If you're planning to visit religious sites like the **Malaga Cathedral** or the **Alcazaba**, make sure to dress modestly (shoulders covered, no shorts) as a sign of respect.

3. Local Customs and Traditions

To get the most out of your trip to Malaga, it's also helpful to understand some of the local customs and traditions that make this Andalusian city unique:

Siesta Time: In many parts of Spain, including Malaga, it's customary to take a **siesta** (afternoon nap) between **2:00 PM and 5:00 PM**. While most businesses stay open during this time, shops and restaurants may close for a couple of hours. This is a great time for a leisurely lunch or a break at a local café.

Flamenco: Flamenco is deeply rooted in Andalusian culture, and Malaga is no exception. If you get the chance, be sure to watch a **flamenco performance**. This passionate, expressive dance is a major part of the region's heritage, and you'll find live flamenco shows at many bars and venues throughout the city.

Semana Santa (Holy Week): Malaga celebrates **Semana Santa** (Holy Week) with a deep sense of tradition and reverence. If you're visiting during **Easter**, you'll witness elaborate processions and ceremonies that reflect the city's deep religious roots. It's a solemn, yet beautiful, experience, and if you decide to participate, remember to be respectful and quiet during processions.

Feria de Agosto: Another major cultural event in Malaga is the **Feria de Agosto**, the summer fair, held in **August**. This week-long festival features traditional music, dancing, and parades. It's a great opportunity to immerse yourself in the local culture, but also a time when the city can get quite lively and crowded.

4. General Travel Etiquette

Punctuality: While Spain is generally laid-back, it's still important to be punctual for any formal appointments, tours, or business meetings. However, for social gatherings and meals, a bit of flexibility with time is often accepted.

Respecting Local Environment: Malaga, like much of Spain, places a high value on preserving the natural beauty of the region. When visiting beaches, parks, or the **Caminito del Rey**, remember to follow the principle of **leave no trace**—dispose of waste properly and respect wildlife.

Smoking: Smoking is still common in many outdoor areas, including **cafés** and **restaurants**, but there are smoking bans in indoor public places. Look for designated smoking areas if you need to light up.

By keeping these cultural norms and etiquette tips in mind, you'll blend in with the locals and truly experience the charm of Malaga. The people here are proud of their culture, so showing respect and making an effort to understand the local way of life will surely be appreciated.

Chapter 10

Eco-Friendly Travel Tips

Traveling is an amazing way to experience new cultures, beautiful landscapes, and incredible history. But as travelers, we also have a responsibility to minimize our impact on the environment. Fortunately, making eco-friendly choices while traveling doesn't have to be complicated or difficult. With a few simple adjustments, you can reduce your carbon footprint, support sustainable businesses, and make a positive impact on the places you visit.

We'll share practical eco-friendly travel tips to help you enjoy your trip while also protecting the planet. These tips will be easy to implement, affordable, and sustainable—because you don't have to sacrifice fun to be eco-conscious.

1. Use Public Transport

In **Malaga**, using public transport is one of the best ways to reduce your environmental impact. The city has an extensive bus and metro network that can take you anywhere from the historic **Alcazaba** to the beautiful beaches. By choosing public transport over taxis or rental cars, you'll cut down on emissions and contribute to cleaner air.

2. Opt for Eco-Friendly Accommodations

Choose accommodations that prioritize sustainability. Many hotels in **Malaga** now focus on eco-friendly practices, such as reducing energy consumption, minimizing waste, and using eco-friendly materials. Some even use renewable energy sources and offer water-saving initiatives.

3. Carry Reusable Bottles and Bags

Plastic waste is a major environmental concern, especially in tourist-heavy areas. Instead of purchasing bottled water or using plastic bags, bring your own reusable items. A reusable water bottle will save you money and prevent plastic waste. Many cafes and restaurants in **Malaga** will even refill your water bottle for free if you ask!

Where to Get Reusable Items:

Carrefour Market: A supermarket chain that offers a variety of eco-friendly and reusable products, including bags and bottles.

- **Address**: Centro Commercial La Rosaleda, Calle Simón Bolivar, s/n, 29011 Málaga, Spain.
- **Phone**: +34 952 61 90 21.

4. Eat Locally and Support Sustainable Restaurants

Support restaurants that focus on local, seasonal, and organic food. By eating locally, you'll be helping reduce the carbon footprint associated with food transportation. In **Malaga**, there are plenty of places offering fresh, locally-sourced meals, many of which also emphasize sustainability.

5. Choose Eco-Tours and Activities

Instead of traditional, larger tours, consider booking eco-friendly activities. **Malaga** has plenty of opportunities to explore nature while minimizing your environmental impact, such as biking tours, hiking trips, or walking tours of the city's historic areas. These low-impact activities not only give you a closer look at the region but also promote sustainable tourism.

Eco-Tour Options:

Malaga Bike Tours: Explore the city by bike with a local guide, taking in the sights while minimizing your carbon footprint.

- **Address**: Plaza Pueto Alfonso Canales, 4, Distrito Centro, 29001 Malaga, Spain.
- **Phone**: +34 650 67 70 63.
- **Website:** https://www.biketoursmalaga.com/

6. Minimize Waste with Digital Tickets and Guides

In an effort to reduce paper waste, opt for digital tickets and guides whenever possible. Many attractions in **Malaga** now offer e-tickets or apps to help you navigate the city. Not only will this save you paper, but it's also much more convenient!

Digital Ticket Options:

Alhambra Palace: The famous **Alhambra** offers e-tickets for visitors to avoid waiting in line and reduce paper waste.

- **Website:** www.alhambra.org

Malaga Museum: The **Museo de Malaga** offers digital tickets for exhibits, allowing you to skip the lines and reduce waste.

- **Website**: https://www.museopicassomalaga.org/en

7. Respect Nature and Local Wildlife

Whether you're hiking through **Caminito del Rey** or visiting the **Nerja Caves**, it's essential to respect the local wildlife and natural environment. Avoid littering, stick to marked trails, and never disturb animals. If you're an animal lover, consider supporting wildlife conservation efforts during your travels.

By making these small, eco-friendly changes, you can enjoy everything **Malaga** has to offer while leaving a minimal impact on the environment. Remember, every choice counts. Whether it's using public transport, supporting sustainable businesses, or choosing eco-friendly activities, your actions can contribute to preserving the beauty of this incredible region for future generations.

Supporting Local Businesses and Communities

When you travel, it's easy to get caught up in the excitement of the sights and sounds around you. But one of the most rewarding ways to experience a destination is by supporting the local businesses and communities. Not only will you be helping the economy, but you'll also get a more authentic and enriching travel experience.

In this chapter, we'll share how you can support local businesses and communities while traveling in **Malaga** and beyond. These tips will help you enjoy your trip in a way that benefits both you and the people you meet along the way.

1. Shop at Local Markets and Artisan Shops

One of the best ways to support local businesses is by buying directly from local artisans and market vendors. In **Malaga**, you'll find a wide range of handmade products, from jewelry and clothing to art and ceramics. Shopping locally allows you to bring home unique souvenirs while also supporting the talented people who create them.

Local Markets in Malaga:

Mercado Atarazanas: A bustling market where you can find fresh produce, seafood, and local delicacies, as well as handmade crafts and products from local artisans.

- **Address**: Calle Atarazanas, 10, 29005 Málaga, Spain.

Malaga Artisan Market: A monthly artisan market held in different locations around **Malaga**, where you can shop for handmade jewelry, artwork, clothing, and more.

- **Location**: Check their website for current locations and dates.
- **Website**: https://visita.malaga.eu/

2. Dine at Locally-Owned Restaurants

Supporting local restaurants is one of the easiest ways to give back to the community. Instead of eating at international chains, look for family-run eateries that serve traditional Andalusian dishes. These restaurants often use fresh, local ingredients, and your meal directly supports the people who prepare it.

3. Stay in Locally-Owned Hotels or Hostels

When choosing where to stay, consider booking with locally-owned accommodations instead of large hotel chains. Local hotels, hostels, and guesthouses often offer more personal service, and your money stays within the community. Plus, you'll get a more authentic experience.

4. Participate in Local Experiences and Tours

Instead of booking large, impersonal tours, look for experiences run by local guides or small businesses. Whether it's a walking tour, cooking class, or wine tasting, local guides can offer insider knowledge and help you connect with the culture on a deeper level. Plus, you'll be supporting a small business owner's livelihood.

5. Support Local Artists and Cultural Institutions

When traveling, it's important to also support local art and culture. Many cities, including **Malaga**, are home to vibrant arts scenes, and visiting local galleries or attending a cultural event can be a great way to help artists and performers.

Local Art Galleries and Museums:

Museo Picasso Málaga: Dedicated to the works of **Pablo Picasso**, the museum showcases his life's work and promotes local art initiatives.

- **Address**: Palacio de Buenavista, Calle San Agustín, 8, 29015 Málaga, Spain.

Museo Carmen Thyssen Málaga: A stunning museum housing a collection of 19th-century Spanish paintings, including works by local artists.

- **Address**: Calle Compañía, 10, 29008 Málaga, Spain.
- **Phone**: +34 952 21 15 11.

Supporting local businesses and communities is a simple yet powerful way to make your travel experience more meaningful. By shopping locally, dining at family-owned restaurants, staying at locally-owned accommodations, and engaging in sustainable activities, you can help improve the local economy and promote ethical travel.

282 | MALAGA TRAVEL GUIDE 2025

Chapter 11

Sample Itineraries for Every Traveler

Málaga is a city of diversity, offering history, culture, culinary experiences, and outdoor adventures. Whether you're in Málaga for a quick visit, a romantic getaway, or a week-long exploration, the city caters to all types of travelers. This chapter provides tailored itineraries to help you make the most of your trip, covering Málaga's rich heritage, coastal beauty, and gastronomic treasures. Let's dive into options for one day, three days, a full week, and specific experiences suited for outdoor enthusiasts, couples, and families.

1-Day Itinerary: A Day Full of Culture, History and Relaxation

If you only have one day to explore Málaga, don't worry—this itinerary will take you through some of the city's most iconic landmarks, delicious dining spots, and relaxing coastal areas. Combining history, culture, and local flavors, it ensures a full and memorable experience in Málaga.

Morning: Exploring Málaga's Historic Core

Start Your Day at the Alcazaba

Begin your morning with a visit to the **Alcazaba**, Málaga's iconic 11th-century Moorish fortress. Stroll through its lush gardens, ancient courtyards, and well-preserved walls while soaking in panoramic views of the city and the harbor. The Alcazaba offers a glimpse into Málaga's Islamic heritage and sets the tone for a culturally rich day.

- **Address**: Calle Alcazabilla, 2, 29012 Málaga, Spain.

Stop by the Roman Theatre

Adjacent to the **Alcazaba**, the **Roman Theatre** is a beautifully preserved reminder of Málaga's Roman past. Walk around the ancient stone seating and imagine how the theater once hosted performances during the Roman Empire. Admission is free, and the site can be easily explored in 15–20 minutes.

- **Address**: Calle Alcazabilla, 8, 29015 Málaga, Spain.

Take a Coffee Break at Café de L'Abuela

Recharge with a quick coffee and pastry at **Café de L'Abuela**, a cozy spot in the heart of the historic center. Known for its fresh, homemade pastries and authentic Spanish coffee, it's the perfect stop before diving into more sightseeing.

- **Address**: Calle Echegaray, 9, 29015 Málaga, Spain.

Visit the Málaga Cathedral

Next, head to **Málaga Cathedral**, an architectural masterpiece known as "La Manquita" due to its unfinished second tower. Admire its intricate Renaissance and Baroque design, explore the interior, and climb to the rooftop for sweeping views of the city and coastline.

- **Address**: Calle Molina Lario, 9, 29015 Málaga, Spain.

Midday: Art and Andalusian Cuisine

Discover the Museo Picasso Málaga

Dedicate part of your midday to visiting the **Museo Picasso Málaga**, located in the **Palacio de Buenavista**. The museum offers an excellent collection of Picasso's works, reflecting the artistic evolution of Málaga's most famous son. Audio guides and temporary exhibitions enrich the experience.

- **Address**: Calle San Agustín, 8, 29015 Málaga, Spain.

Enjoy Lunch at El Mesón de Cervantes

For lunch, visit **El Mesón de Cervantes**, a highly recommended restaurant offering a range of Spanish tapas with a modern twist. Dishes like Iberian pork cheek or traditional **ajoblanco (chilled almond soup)** are crowd favorites, and the wine selection is excellent.

- **Address**: Calle Álamos, 11, 29012 Málaga, Spain.
- **Phone**: +34 952 21 62 74.

Afternoon: Coastal Views and Local Life

Walk Along Muelle Uno

After lunch, take a leisurely stroll along **Muelle Uno**, Málaga's modern waterfront promenade. The area offers shops, open-air art installations, and views of the yachts docked in the marina. Stop at the **Centre Pompidou Málaga**, a cultural hub for modern art lovers. Its cube-shaped building is a landmark, and the exhibitions are thought-provoking.

- **Muelle Uno Address**: Puerto de Málaga, 4, 29016 Málaga, Spain.
- **Centre Pompidou Málaga Address**: Pasaje Doctor Carrillo Casaux, s/n, Muelle Uno, 29016 Málaga, Spain.

Relax at Playa de la Malagueta

No visit to Málaga is complete without some time by the sea. Head to **Playa de la Malagueta**, the city's closest beach, to unwind. Pack a towel, take a walk along the sandy shores, or dip your feet into the Mediterranean waters. If you're craving a snack, try grilled sardines at a nearby **chiringuito (beach bar).**

- **Address**: Paseo Marítimo Pablo Ruiz Picasso, 29016 Málaga, Spain.

Evening: Sunset and Dinner

Catch the Sunset at Gibralfaro Viewpoint

As the day winds down, take a taxi or walk up to the **Gibralfaro Viewpoint**, where you can enjoy one of the best sunset views in

Málaga. Overlooking the harbor, the **Alcazaba**, and the city, this spot is a photographer's dream.

- **Address**: Camino Gibralfaro, 11, 29016 Málaga, Spain.

Dinner at Restaurante Amador

End your day with an unforgettable dining experience at **Restaurante Amador**, located in the **Hotel Villa Guadalupe**. Known for its innovative take on Andalusian cuisine, the restaurant also boasts stunning views of the city at night. Try the slow-cooked lamb or seafood paella, paired with a local wine.

- **Address**: Calle Bandaneira, 6, 29190 Málaga, Spain.
- **Phone**: +34 952 43 28 62.

This carefully planned one-day itinerary ensures you experience Málaga's historical landmarks, artistic heritage, coastal beauty, and culinary delights. It's designed to give first-time visitors a memorable and well-rounded introduction to the heart of the Costa del Sol.

3-Day Itinerary: Discovering the Best of Malaga

If you're visiting **Malaga** for the first time and only have three days to explore, don't worry—there's plenty to see, do, and experience in this beautiful city. From rich cultural landmarks to stunning beaches and delicious food, **Malaga** has something for everyone.

Here's a simple and easy-to-follow 3-day itinerary that will help you discover the best of **Malaga**, all while taking in its history, lively atmosphere, and local culture.

Day 1: Explore the Historic Heart of Malaga

Morning:

Start your first day by diving right into the historic core of **Malaga**. You'll be walking through centuries of history in a small, easily walkable area. Begin at **Plaza de la Constitución**, the central square, where you'll see cafes, shops, and beautiful architecture.

- **Address**: Plaza de la Constitución, 29005 Málaga, Spain.

From here, head over to **Calle Larios**, an exciting shopping street lined with stores and historical buildings. It's one of the most famous pedestrian streets in **Malaga**.

- **Address**: Calle Larios, 29005 Málaga, Spain.

Next, make your way to the **Alcazaba**, an 11th-century Moorish fortress that offers stunning views of the city and the sea. It's one of **Malaga's** most iconic landmarks.

- **Address**: Calle Alcazabilla, 2, 29012 Málaga, Spain.

Lunch break:

After all that walking, stop for lunch at a traditional Andalusian restaurant. **El Pimpi** is a local favorite for both its delicious food and its warm atmosphere.

- **Address**: Calle Granada, 62, 29015 Málaga, Spain.

Afternoon

After lunch, visit the **Museo Picasso Málaga** to see the works of **Pablo Picasso**, one of the most famous artists in the world who was born in **Malaga**. This museum is not only a must-see for art lovers, but also offers a glimpse into the life and artistic development of Picasso.

- **Address**: Palacio de Buenavista, Calle San Agustín, 8, 29015 Málaga, Spain.

End your day with a leisurely walk along **La Malagueta Beach**, just a short stroll from the museum. You can relax, take in the sunset, and enjoy the ocean breeze.

- **Address**: Paseo Marítimo Pablo Ruiz Picasso, 29016 Málaga, Spain.

Day 2: Dive into Culture and History

Morning:

On day two, visit the **Gibralfaro Castle**. Perched high on a hill, this castle offers breathtaking panoramic views of **Malaga**. It's the perfect place to start your day. The walk up to the castle can be a little steep, but it's absolutely worth it.

- **Address**: Camino Gibralfaro, 11, 29016 Málaga, Spain.

After visiting the castle, head back down to the city to check out **the Roman Theatre**. This ancient landmark is a beautiful example of Roman architecture and lies just below the **Alcazaba**.

- **Address**: Calle Alcazabilla, 8, 29015 Málaga, Spain.

Lunch break:

For lunch, make your way to **La Tranca**, a cozy spot where you can enjoy local tapas. This place is popular among locals and is perfect for trying traditional dishes like **tortilla española** or **ensalada malagueña**.

- **Address**: Calle Carretería, 92, 29008 Málaga, Spain.

Afternoon:

In the afternoon, head to the **Museo Carmen Thyssen Málaga**, a beautiful art museum housed in a former palace. Here, you'll find a rich collection of 19th-century Spanish paintings, focusing on Andalusian artists.

- **Address**: Calle Compañía, 10, 29008 Málaga, Spain.

Afterward, take a stroll through the **Jardín Botánico-Histórico La Concepción**, a historical botanical garden just a short distance from the city center. The lush greenery and peaceful surroundings will provide a relaxing break from the bustle of the city.

- **Address**: Camino del Jardin Botanico, 3, 29014 Málaga, Spain.

Day 3: Enjoy the Coastal Beauty of Malaga

Morning:

On your last day, start by visiting the **Muelle Uno** shopping and dining complex by the harbor. It's a great spot to shop for local products or just enjoy the sea views. You can also check out the nearby **Centre Pompidou Málaga**, which is part of the famous French museum chain and houses modern art exhibitions.

- **Muelle Uno Address**: Puerto de Málaga, 4, 29016 Málaga, Spain.
- **Centre Pompidou Málaga Address**: Pasaje Doctor Carrillo Casaux, s/n, Muelle Uno, 29016 Málaga, Spain.

Lunch break:

For lunch, head to **El Tintero**, an iconic seafood restaurant where waiters bring fresh seafood to your table and you can pick whatever catches your eye. It's an unforgettable dining experience.

- **Address**: Avenue Salvador Allende, 340, Malaga-Este, 29017 Málaga, Spain.

Afternoon:

Spend your afternoon at **Malaga's beaches**. Whether you're relaxing at **Playa de la Malagueta**, **Playa del Palo**, or **Playa de Pedregalejo**, you'll enjoy the warm Mediterranean waters and a laid-back atmosphere.

End your trip with a sunset walk along the **Paseo Marítimo**—a lovely beachfront promenade where you can reflect on the beautiful memories you've made in **Malaga**.

- **Address**: Paseo Marítimo, 29016 Málaga, Spain.

This 3-day itinerary gives you a perfect blend of culture, history, nature, and relaxation, ensuring that you experience the best of ***Malaga***.

MALAGA CATHEDRAL

SCAN THE QR CODE

295 | MALAGA TRAVEL GUIDE 2025

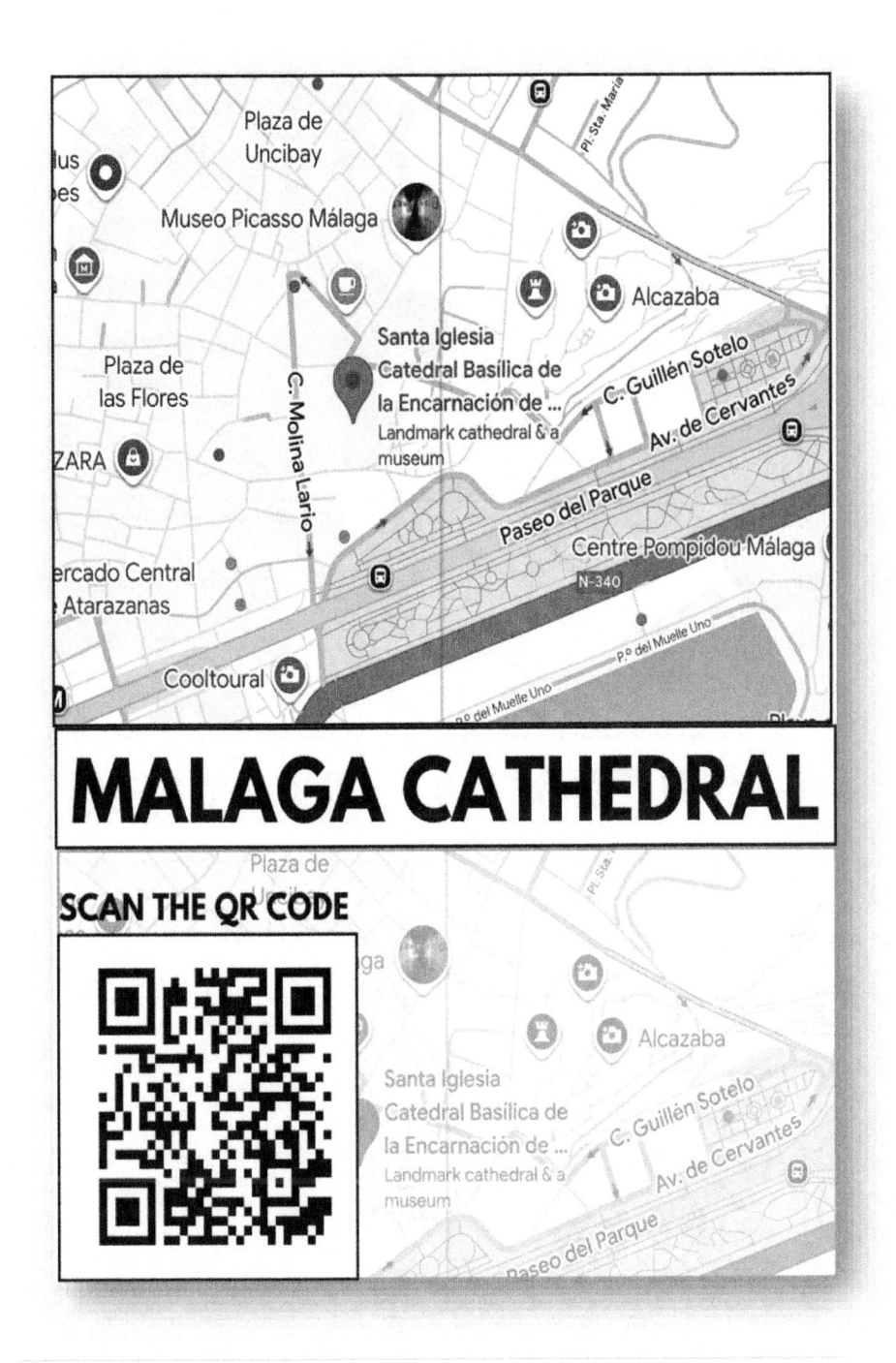

MERCADO ATARAZANAS

SCAN THE QR CODE

296 | MALAGA TRAVEL GUIDE 2025

7-Day Itinerary: A Deeper Dive into Malaga and the Costa del Sol

If you have a week to spend in **Malaga** and want to explore not just the city itself, but also the beautiful **Costa del Sol**, this itinerary is for you. You'll get a deeper experience of the region's history, culture, and natural beauty. From exploring historic sites to relaxing on stunning beaches, this trip will make the most of your time in **Malaga**.

Day 1: Discover the Historic Heart of Malaga

Morning:

Kickstart your adventure with a visit to the **Alcazaba**, one of **Malaga's** most iconic landmarks. This Moorish fortress offers panoramic views of the city and a deep dive into **Malaga's** Islamic past. Spend time wandering through its beautiful gardens and ancient halls.

- **Address**: Calle Alcazabilla, 2, 29012 Málaga, Spain.

Afterward, head to the **Roman Theatre**, just at the foot of the Alcazaba. It's a quiet spot but a fascinating piece of history. Take your time to admire the preserved ruins and imagine what it would have been like when it was used for performances centuries ago.

- **Address**: Calle Alcazabilla, 8, 29015 Málaga, Spain.

Lunch break:

For lunch, enjoy a delicious plate of traditional Andalusian food at **El Pimpi**, a local favorite. The restaurant has a warm, welcoming atmosphere and serves authentic tapas that reflect **Malaga's** culinary culture.

- **Address**: Calle Granada, 62, 29015 Málaga, Spain.

Afternoon:

In the afternoon, head to the **Museo Picasso Málaga**. Picasso was born in **Malaga**, and this museum offers a deep dive into his early years and his artistic evolution. It's a must-see for art lovers.

- **Address**: Palacio de Buenavista, Calle San Agustín, 8, 29015 Málaga, Spain.

End your day by taking a stroll down **Calle Larios**, **Malaga's** main shopping street. It's a lively area with a mix of high-end shops, local boutiques, and charming cafes.

- **Address**: Calle Larios, 29005 Málaga, Spain.

Day 2: A Trip to the Beach and Coastal Views

Morning:

Start your day by visiting **La Malagueta Beach**. Just a short walk from the city center, this beach is perfect for a relaxing morning by the sea. You can take a swim, relax on the sand, or simply enjoy a coffee at one of the beachfront cafes.

- **Address**: Paseo Marítimo Pablo Ruiz Picasso, 29016 Málaga, Spain.

After the beach, head to the nearby **Gibralfaro Castle**. This castle offers one of the best views in **Malaga**, and you'll learn about the city's military history. The walk up can be steep, but it's definitely worth the effort.

- **Address**: Camino Gibralfaro, 11, 29016 Málaga, Spain.

Lunch break:

After a morning of sightseeing, enjoy a fresh seafood lunch at **El Tintero**. Known for its traditional Spanish seafood dishes, you'll love the lively atmosphere as waiters bring fresh fish to your table for you to choose from.

- **Address**: Avenue Salvador Allende, 340, Malaga-Este, 29017 Málaga, Spain.

Afternoon:

In the afternoon, spend some time exploring the **Jardín Botánico-Histórico La Concepción**, one of the most beautiful botanical gardens in the region. It's a peaceful escape from the city where you can explore lush greenery and enjoy the natural beauty of the area.

- **Address**: Camino del Jardin Botanico, 3, 29014 Málaga, Spain.

Day 3: Day Trip to Ronda

Morning:

On day three, take a day trip to **Ronda**, a beautiful town located about 1.5 hours from **Malaga**. Famous for its dramatic cliffs and historic bridges, **Ronda** is one of the most picturesque towns in Spain. Start your visit at the **Puente Nuevo**, the stunning bridge that spans the **Tajo Gorge**.

Puente Nuevo: One of **Ronda's** most iconic landmarks.

- **Address**: Pl. Espana, 29400 Ronda, Málaga, Spain

From here, wander through the old town of **Ronda**, exploring its narrow streets and beautiful whitewashed buildings. Don't forget to visit the **Plaza de Toros**, one of the oldest bullrings in Spain.

- o **Address**: C. Virgen de la Paz, 15, 29400 Ronda, Málaga, Spain.

Lunch break:

Enjoy a traditional meal at **Restaurante Pedro Romero**, which offers fantastic Andalusian cuisine and views of the town. It's a great place to relax and recharge before continuing your exploration of **Ronda**.

- o **Address**: C. Virgen de la Paz, 18, 29400 Ronda, Málaga, Spain.

Afternoon:

Spend your afternoon exploring the **Banos Arabes**, the historic Arab baths that have been beautifully preserved. This site gives you a glimpse into **Ronda's** Moorish past.

Banos Arabes: Discover **Ronda's** Moorish heritage.

- o **Address**: Calle Molino, s/n, 29400 Ronda, Málaga, Spain.

Day 4: Marbella and Puerto Banus

Morning:

On day four, take a day trip to **Marbella**, located just a short drive from **Malaga**. Start with a stroll through **Marbella Old Town**, a charming area with narrow cobblestone streets, whitewashed houses, and lively cafes. **Plaza de los Naranjos** is the perfect spot to begin your visit.

- **Address**: Calle Peral 4, 29600, Marbella, Spain.

From the old town, head to the nearby **Puerto Banus** marina. This glamorous area is known for luxury yachts, high-end boutiques, and celebrity sightings.

- **Address**: Nueva Andalucia, 29660 Marbella, Málaga, Spain.

Lunch break:

For lunch, enjoy a seafood meal at **Restaurante El Ancla** in **Puerto Banus**. It's a fantastic spot for fresh seafood, with a view of the marina.

Restaurante El Ancla: Seafood with a view of the marina.

- **Address**: Avenue Carmen Sevilla, 29670 Marbella, Málaga, Spain

Afternoon:

Spend the rest of your afternoon exploring **Puerto Banus** or relax on the beaches in **Marbella**. Enjoy the Mediterranean sun and the lively atmosphere of the area.

Day 5: Malaga's Modern Attractions and Relaxation

Morning:

On your fifth day, start your day by visiting the **Centre Pompidou Málaga**, a branch of the famous Parisian museum. Located in the port area, it's a must-visit for modern art enthusiasts.

- **Address**: Pasaje Doctor Carrillo Casaux, s/n, Muelle Uno, 29016 Málaga, Spain.

Lunch break:

For lunch, enjoy a meal at **El Refectorium**, a stylish restaurant offering a modern take on Andalusian cuisine. It's a great way to experience traditional flavors with a contemporary twist.

El Refectorium: A stylish spot for modern Andalusian cuisine.

- **Address**: Calle Cervantes, 8, 29016 Málaga, Spain

Afternoon:

Explore the **Atarazanas Market**, Málaga's historic central market. Sample local delicacies like fresh olives, Iberian ham, and seafood.

- **Address**: Calle Atarazanas, 10, 29005 Málaga, Spain.

Day 6: Hiking and Nature

Morning:

Take a day trip to the **Caminito del Rey**, a stunning walkway along cliffs and gorges. This thrilling hike offers incredible views of the **Guadalhorce River**.

- **Address**: Caminito del Rey, El Chorro, 29550 Ardales, Málaga, Spain.

Lunch break:

Have lunch at **Restaurante El Mirador**, located near the trail, offering hearty Spanish dishes and panoramic views.

- **Address:** Parque de Ardales, Zona Cuarta, 29552 Ardales, Málaga, Spain.

Afternoon:

After lunch, visit the **El Chorro reservoir** for a relaxing stroll or a paddleboat ride. Return to Málaga in the evening.

- **Address:** Pantana del Chorro, 29320.

Day 7: Relaxation and Farewell

Morning:

Spend your final morning unwinding at **Playa del Palo**, a quiet beach ideal for swimming and relaxing.

- **Address**: Calle Banda del Mar, 29017 Málaga, Spain.

Lunch break:

Enjoy a farewell meal at **Restaurante Amador**, located in **Hotel Villa Guadalupe**. The panoramic views of Málaga and innovative dishes make it a perfect way to end your trip.

- **Address**: Calle Bandaneira, 6, 29190 Málaga, Spain.

Afternoon:

Take a leisurely walk along the **Paseo Marítimo**, reflecting on your week in Málaga as you enjoy the sea breeze.

This **7-day itinerary** *offers a perfect balance of history, culture, outdoor activities, and relaxation, ensuring you make the most of your time in Málaga and the Costa del Sol.*

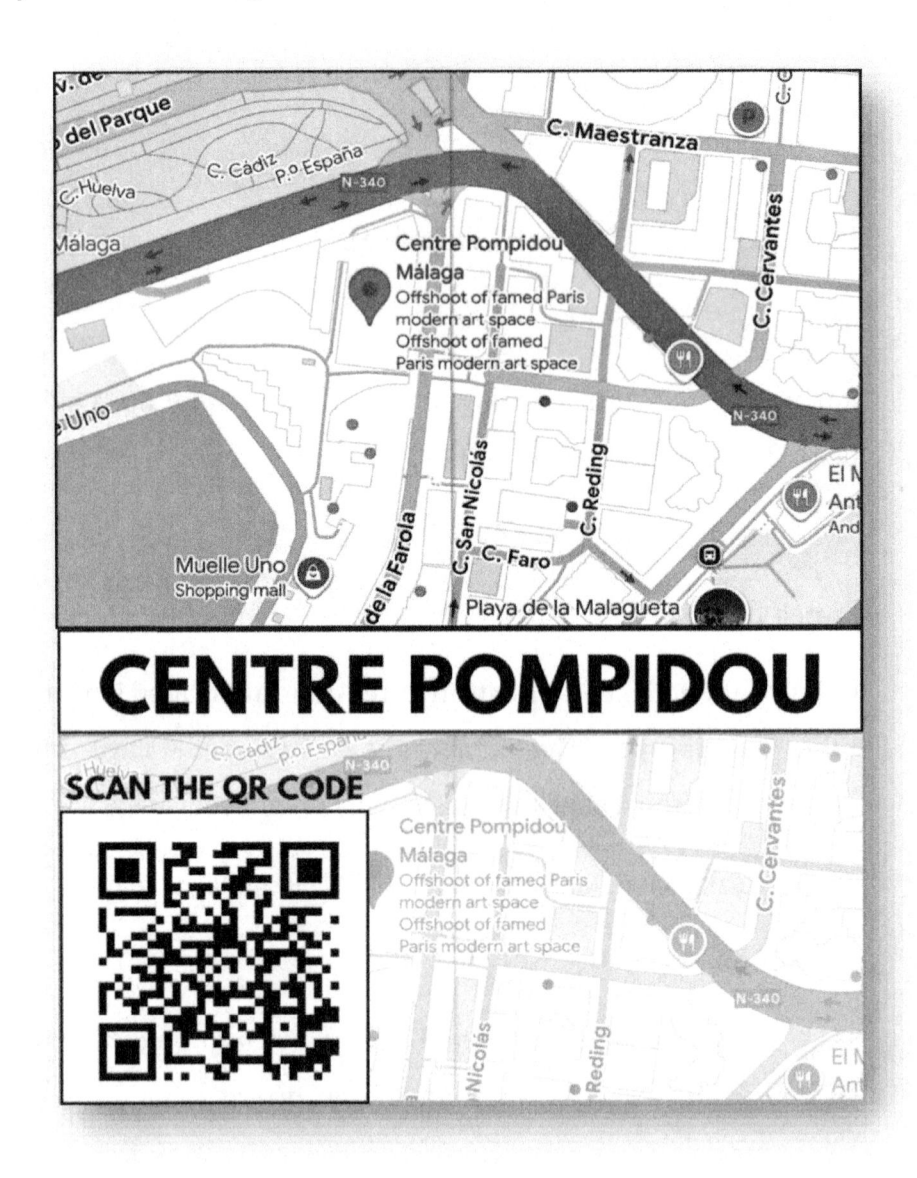

CENTRE POMPIDOU

SCAN THE QR CODE

MUSEO CARMEN THYSSEN

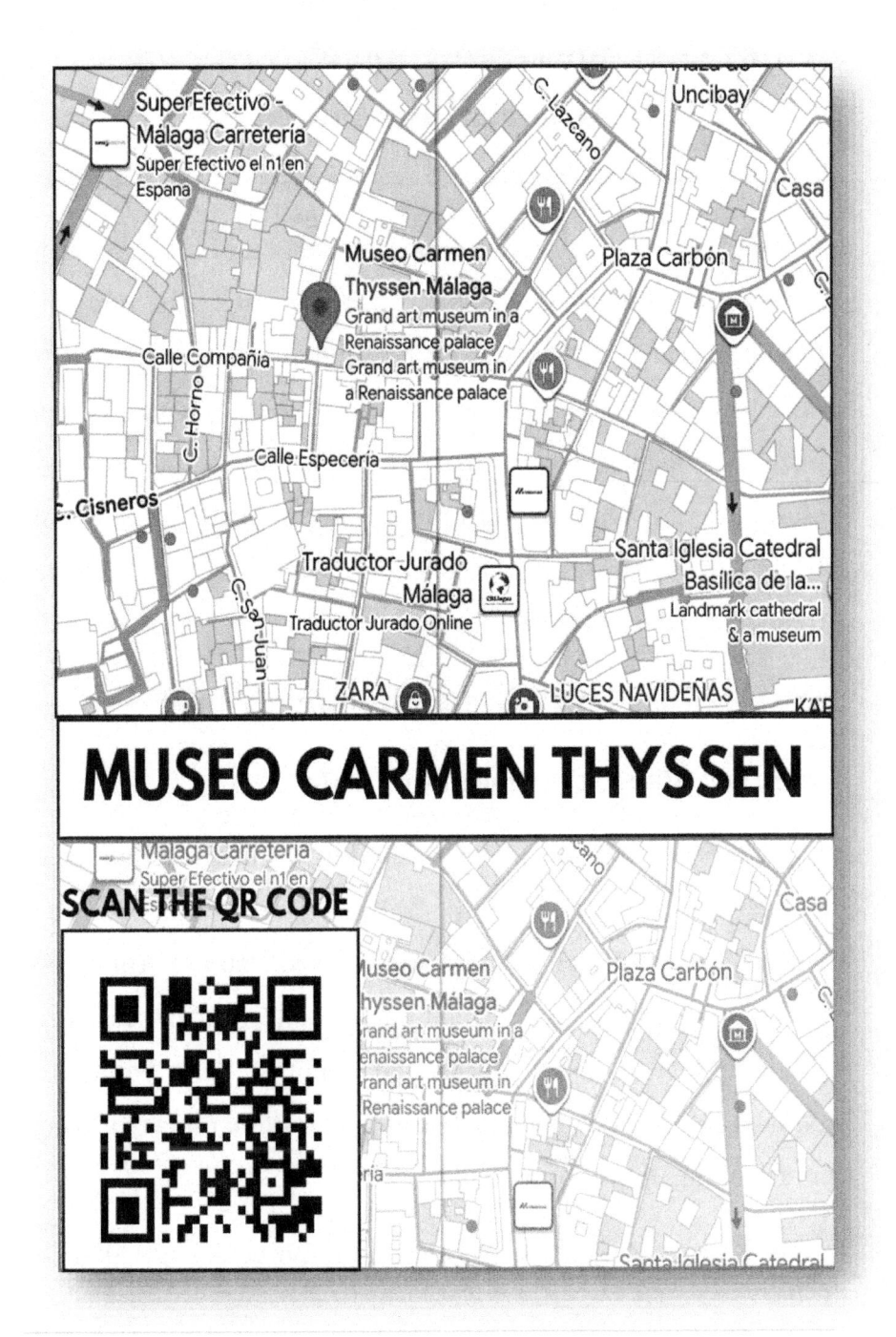

SCAN THE QR CODE

307 | MALAGA TRAVEL GUIDE 2025

3-Day Outdoor Lovers and Nature Enthusiasts Itinerary in Malaga

For those who love the outdoors, Málaga and its surrounding areas offer breathtaking landscapes, coastal trails, and lush gardens. This 3-day itinerary is designed for nature lovers and outdoor enthusiasts who want to connect with Málaga's natural beauty while experiencing its cultural essence. From hiking and stunning viewpoints to tranquil botanical gardens and scenic beaches, this carefully crafted itinerary ensures your days are filled with adventure and discovery.

Day 1: Hills, Gardens, and Stunning Views

Morning: Hike to the Gibralfaro Castle

tart your outdoor adventure with a hike to **Gibralfaro Castle**, perched on a hill overlooking Málaga. The walk is steep but rewarding, with panoramic views of the city, harbor, and coastline. Along the way, you'll pass Mediterranean pine trees and scenic viewpoints perfect for photos. Take your time enjoying the castle grounds, learning about its military history, and soaking in the stunning vistas.

- **Address**: Camino Gibralfaro, 11, 29016 Málaga, Spain.

Midday: Explore the Jardín Botánico-Histórico La Concepción

After your hike, head to the **Jardín Botánico-Histórico La Concepción**, one of Europe's most beautiful botanical gardens. Wander through tropical plants, cascading waterfalls, and shaded trails. Don't miss the **Wisteria Walk**, the **Bamboo Forest**, and the historic lookout point with views of Málaga's skyline. This peaceful haven is ideal for outdoor enthusiasts who enjoy exploring diverse plant life.

- **Address**: Camino del Jardín Botánico, 3, 29014 Málaga, Spain.

Lunch break: El Pimpi Florida

Recharge with lunch at **El Pimpi Florida**, a hidden gem in the El Palo district. Known for its rustic ambiance and locally-sourced ingredients, this spot serves authentic Andalusian dishes, including seafood and vegetarian options.

- **Address**: Calle Almeria, 13, 29018 Málaga, Spain.

Afternoon: Paseo del Parque and Muelle Uno

Spend your afternoon strolling through **Paseo del Parque**, a lush park filled with tropical plants and shaded walkways. From here, continue to **Muelle Uno**, Málaga's waterfront promenade. Enjoy the fresh sea breeze and views of the Mediterranean.

- **Paseo del Parque Address**: Paseo del Parque, 29015 Málaga, Spain.
- **Muelle Uno Address**: Puerto del Muelle Uno, 4, 29016 Málaga, Spain.

Day 2: Trails, Forests, and Coastal Serenity

Morning: Montes de Málaga Natural Park

Dedicate the morning to exploring the **Montes de Málaga Natural Park**, located just 20 minutes from the city center. This sprawling park is perfect for hiking, with trails that wind through pine forests, valleys, and streams. Popular routes include the **Sendero Torrijos** and **Sendero El Cerrado**, both offering beautiful landscapes and opportunities to spot wildlife like birds and deer.

- **Address**: Parque Natural Montes de Málaga, 29013 Málaga, Spain.
- **Visitor Center**: Cortijo de Torrijos.

Lunch break: Restaurante Venta El Detalle

Stop for lunch at **Restaurante Venta El Detalle**, a family-run restaurant near the park that serves traditional dishes like slow-cooked stews and grilled meats. Pair your meal with a glass of local Málaga wine.

- **Address**: A-7000, 20, 29193 Málaga, Spain.

Afternoon: Relax at Playa del Palo

Return to Málaga and unwind at **Playa del Palo**, a quieter beach perfect for swimming or strolling along the shore. This beach is frequented by locals and has a relaxed, authentic atmosphere.

- **Address**: Calle Banda del Mar, 29017 Málaga, Spain.

Dinner: Enjoy Seafood at Restaurante El Tintero

Conclude your day with dinner at **Restaurante El Tintero**, where waiters serve fresh seafood dishes in a fun and casual setting by the sea.

- **Address**: Avenida Salvador Allende, 340, 29017 Málaga, Spain.

Day 3: Dramatic Cliffs and Coastal Trails

Morning: Caminito del Rey

Experience one of Spain's most famous outdoor attractions: the **Caminito del Rey**, a stunning cliffside walkway through the **El**

Chorro Gorge. This 7.7-km trail offers incredible views of dramatic cliffs, turquoise waters, and verdant landscapes. Walk along suspended pathways, cross the glass-bottom bridge, and marvel at the engineering behind this thrilling trail. Tickets must be booked in advance.

- **Address**: Caminito del Rey, 29550, Ardales, Málaga, Spain.

Lunch break: Restaurante El Mirador

After completing the trail, enjoy lunch at **Restaurante El Mirador**, located near the entrance of Caminito del Rey. This restaurant offers stunning views of the surrounding landscape and serves hearty Andalusian dishes.

- **Address**: Parque de Ardales, Zona Cuarta, 29552, Ardales, Málaga, Spain.

Afternoon: Pinar del Rey Forest

On your way back to Málaga, make a stop at **Pinar del Rey**, a tranquil forest perfect for an afternoon walk or a short hike. The trails here wind through lush pine forests and lead to scenic picnic spots.

- **Address**: Carretera Pinar del Rey, 11360 San Roque, Málaga, Spain.

Dinner: Wrap Up Your Adventure at La Deriva

End your trip with a delicious meal at **La Deriva**, a contemporary restaurant offering a creative take on traditional Andalusian flavors. Reflect on your outdoor adventures as you savor dishes made from fresh, local ingredients.

- **Address**: Alameda de Colón, 7, 29001 Málaga, Spain.

This 3-day itinerary showcases Málaga's stunning natural beauty and outdoor experiences, ensuring an unforgettable trip for nature enthusiasts. From mountain hikes to coastal relaxation, every moment will leave you feeling inspired and connected to the region's remarkable landscapes.

3-Day Romantic Getaway Itinerary: Discovering the Most Romantic Side of Malaga

Málaga offers couples a blend of rich cultural experiences, serene coastal beauty, and delicious Andalusian cuisine. This 3-day romantic getaway itinerary is designed to create lasting memories for you and your partner while exploring the best the city has to offer. From breathtaking views to cozy dining spots, this carefully crafted itinerary will ensure a memorable escape.

Day 1: Romantic Strolls and Historic Discoveries

Morning:

Start your romantic getaway with a visit to **Plaza de la Constitución**, the beating heart of Málaga's Old Town. This central square is perfect for a peaceful morning stroll as you admire the historic buildings and soak in the local atmosphere.

- **Address**: Plaza de la Constitución, 29005 Málaga, Spain.

From there, walk hand in hand down **Calle Larios**, Málaga's most elegant pedestrian street. Take your time to browse boutique stores or enjoy a coffee together at one of the street-side cafes.

Next, visit the **Alcazaba**, an 11th-century Moorish fortress with beautiful gardens, peaceful courtyards, and spectacular views of the city and sea. Spend time exploring this iconic site and enjoy the tranquil atmosphere as you imagine life here centuries ago.

- **Address**: Calle Alcazabilla, 2, 29012 Málaga, Spain.

Lunch break:

Dine at **Restaurante El Jardín**, a romantic restaurant with a tranquil garden setting near **Málaga Cathedral**. Savor dishes like seafood paella or Andalusian-style pork while enjoying the ambiance of its intimate outdoor patio.

- **Address**: Avenue del Prado, 29660, Marbella, Málaga.

Afternoon:

Spend the afternoon at the **Museo Picasso Málaga**, celebrating Málaga's most famous son, **Pablo Picasso**. The serene atmosphere and stunning artwork make it a perfect setting for a quiet and contemplative experience with your partner.

- **Address**: Calle San Agustín, 8, 29015 Málaga, Spain

Evening:

End your day with a sunset stroll along **La Malagueta Beach**, where you can enjoy the gentle sea breeze and the orange glow of the Mediterranean sunset. Stop for a cocktail at a beachfront bar like **Chiringuito Tropicana** before heading to dinner.

- **Address**: Playa de la Malagueta, Paseo Marítimo Pablo Ruiz Picasso, 29016 Málaga, Spain.

Dinner:

Dine at **Restaurante Amador**, an intimate restaurant located in the hills with spectacular nighttime views of Málaga's city lights. Try their tasting menu, which features Andalusian dishes with a modern twist, and toast to your first romantic day in Málaga.

- **Address**: Calle Bandaneira, 6, 29190 Málaga, Spain.

Day 2: Discovering Málaga's Culture and Nature

Morning:

Start your day at **Gibralfaro Castle**, a hilltop fortress offering unparalleled views of the coastline and the city below. Walk along the castle walls with your partner, enjoying the early morning tranquility. It's also a great spot to take romantic photos and share quiet moments.

- **Address**: Camino Gibralfaro, 11, 29016 Málaga, Spain.

Midday:

Make your way down to the **Roman Theatre**, located just below the Alcazaba. Stroll through the ancient ruins, imagining the stories that unfolded there centuries ago.

- **Address**: Calle Alcazabilla, 8, 29015 Málaga, Spain.

Lunch break:

Enjoy lunch at **La Deriva**, a stylish restaurant with a serene atmosphere perfect for couples. Choose from their selection of fresh seafood and traditional Andalusian dishes with a contemporary twist.

- **Address**: Alameda de Colón, 7, 29001 Malaga, Spain.

Afternoon:

Take a peaceful break at the **Jardín Botánico-Histórico La Concepción**, a serene botanical garden located just outside the city. Explore its shaded pathways, hidden waterfalls, and tropical plants, making it a perfect spot for a romantic escape from the city.

- **Address**: Camino del Jardin Botanico, 3, 29014 Málaga, Spain.

Dinner:

For dinner, reserve a table at **Restaurante Vino Mío**, located near Plaza de la Merced. This cozy spot features fusion dishes and often includes live flamenco performances in the evenings, adding a touch of Andalusian passion to your night.

- **Address**: Plaza Jerónimo Cuervo, 2, 29012 Málaga, Spain.

Day 3: Coastal Beauty and Waterfront Romance

Morning:

Start your final day at **Muelle Uno**, Málaga's bustling port area. Shop for unique souvenirs at local boutiques, take a walk by the harbor, and enjoy the fresh sea air.

- **Address**: Puerto del Muelle Uno, 4, 29016 Málaga, Spain.

After that, visit the nearby **Centre Pompidou Málaga**, an extension of the famous Parisian museum. The colorful cube-shaped building is hard to miss, and the museum houses an impressive collection of contemporary art.

- **Address**: Pasaje Doctor Carrillo Casaux, s/n, Muelle Uno, 29016 Málaga, Spain.

Lunch break:

For lunch, visit **El Tintero**, a lively seafood restaurant known for its unique service style where waiters announce dishes and you pick what you'd like. It's a fun and memorable dining experience for couples.

- **Address:** Avenida Salvador Allende, 340, 29017 Málaga, Spain.

Afternoon:

Spend your final afternoon relaxing on **Playa de Pedregalejo**, one of Málaga's most romantic beaches. Known for its tranquil atmosphere, this beach offers plenty of cozy spots to relax or enjoy a swim together.

- **Address**: Avenida Juan Sebastián Elcano, 29017 Málaga, Spain.

Sunset and Dinner:

Conclude your romantic getaway with a sunset catamaran cruise departing from **Marina del Este**. Sip on champagne and watch the sun dip below the horizon, creating the perfect ending to your Málaga trip.

Afterward, have dinner at **Restaurante José Carlos García**, a Michelin-starred restaurant located on Muelle Uno. With its sophisticated ambiance and innovative cuisine, it's the ultimate spot to celebrate your time together.

- **Address**: Plaza de la Capilla, Puerto de Málaga, 1, 29016 Málaga, Spain.

This 3-day romantic getaway itinerary is designed to help you and your partner experience the best of Málaga while creating meaningful and lasting memories. From cultural landmarks to serene gardens and intimate dining experiences, Málaga is the perfect destination for romance.

5-Day Family-Friendly Itinerary: A Curated Itinerary for Traveling with Kids

Traveling with kids can be an exciting yet challenging experience. But don't worry, **Malaga** offers plenty of activities to keep everyone entertained. From hands-on museums to beautiful parks and beaches, there's something for the whole family to enjoy. This itinerary is designed to help you make the most of your family trip to **Malaga**, with easy, fun, and educational experiences for all ages.

Day 1: Exploring Malaga's Cultural Sights

Morning:

Start your day with a visit to **Alcazaba**, a historic fortress that kids will love to explore. With its stone walls, gardens, and sweeping views of the city, it's the perfect introduction to **Malaga's** rich history. The ramparts are a great place to let kids roam around, and there are even some interactive displays to make learning fun.

- **Address**: Calle Alcazabilla, 2, 29012 Málaga, Spain.

Lunch break:

For lunch, stop by **Bodeguita El Gallo**, a family-friendly spot that serves traditional Spanish food with a relaxed atmosphere. The kids will love the tapas, and the parents can enjoy some local specialties while taking a break from sightseeing.

- **Address**: Calle Cuarteles, 12, 29002 Málaga, Spain.

Afternoon:

After lunch, head to **Museo Interactivo de la Música** (Interactive Music Museum). This museum is a hit with families because it allows kids to play real instruments and learn about music in a hands-on way. There are fun exhibits, interactive displays, and even workshops designed for young visitors.

- **Address**: Calle Beatas, 15, 29008 Málaga, Spain.

Day 2: Beach Fun and Outdoor Adventures

Morning:

No visit to **Malaga** is complete without a trip to **La Malagueta Beach**. This family-friendly beach has calm waters, making it perfect for young children. Spend your morning building sandcastles, splashing in the water, or simply relaxing by the sea. There are also plenty of cafes along the beach for a refreshing drink.

- **Address**: Playa de la Malagueta, Paseo Marítimo Pablo Ruiz Picasso, 29016 Málaga, Spain.

Lunch break:

Enjoy a family-friendly lunch at **Casa Lola**, a lively restaurant offering traditional Andalusian tapas. The kids will love the bite-sized dishes, and the menu caters to a variety of tastes.

- **Address**: Calle Granada, 46, 29015 Málaga, Spain.

Afternoon:

After the beach, take a short drive to the **Parque de la Paloma**, a huge park filled with lakes, playgrounds, and animals. The kids can enjoy feeding the ducks, playing on the swings, or having a picnic in the large green spaces. The park is perfect for a leisurely afternoon of family fun.

- **Address**: Av. Federico Garcia Lorca, 29630, Málaga, Spain.

Day 3: Adventure and Nature Exploration

Morning:

Spend the morning at the **Bioparc Fuengirola**, just a short drive from **Malaga**. This is a fantastic zoo that focuses on conservation and allows visitors to walk through recreations of natural habitats. The kids will be amazed by the animals and enjoy getting close to creatures like gorillas, tigers, and exotic birds.

- **Address**: Calle Camilo José Cela, 6 y 8, 29640 Fuengirola, Málaga, Spain.

Lunch break:

Stop for lunch at **Restaurante Casa Tua**, a cozy spot where the family can enjoy delicious homemade Italian dishes. The warm, welcoming environment is perfect for a midday break.

- **Address**: Calle Virgen del Pilar, 17, 29602, Marbella, Málaga, Spain.

Afternoon:

In the afternoon, visit the **Caminito del Rey**, a thrilling walk along a narrow pathway suspended above a gorge. The kids will love the adventure, and the views are absolutely stunning. However, this is best for older kids, as it requires a bit of physical stamina.

- **Address**: Carretera MA-5403, El Chorro, 29550 Ardales, Málaga, Spain.

Alternative for Younger Kids: Parque de Málaga

If the Caminito del Rey isn't suitable, spend the morning at **Parque de Málaga**, a large park with shaded paths, playgrounds, and fountains where kids can run around.

- **Address**: Paseo del Parque, 29015 Málaga, Spain.

Day 4: A Day of Fun at Amusement Parks

Morning:

Head to **Tivoli World** in **Benalmádena**, just 30 minutes from **Malaga**. This amusement park has rides and attractions for kids of all ages, from gentle carousels to thrilling roller coasters. There's also a kids' zone with fun games and activities.

- **Address**: Avenida Manantial, 1, 29631 Benalmádena, Málaga, Spain.

Lunch break:

For lunch, enjoy some snacks and light bites at the park's **Snack Bar**, where you'll find kid-friendly options like pizza, sandwiches, and ice cream.

- **Address**: Tivoli World, Avenida Manantial, 1, 29631 Benalmádena, Málaga, Spain.

Afternoon:

Spend the afternoon at **Parque del Oeste**, a family-friendly park with playgrounds, ponds, and even a few exotic animals like peacocks and wallabies. It's the perfect place to relax and let the kids play before heading home.

- **Address**: C. Realanga de San Luis, 11, Carretera de Cadiz, 29004, Malaga, Spain.

Day 5: A Relaxing Day in Malaga

Morning:

On your final day, enjoy a relaxing morning at the **Jardín Botánico-Histórico La Concepción**. This botanical garden is a peaceful escape, with beautiful flowers, ponds, and shady paths where the kids can run around safely.

- **Address**: Camino del Jardin Botanico, 3, 29014 Málaga, Spain.

Lunch break:

For lunch, head to **Restaurante El Refectorium**. It's a wonderful spot for a relaxed meal with a variety of family-friendly dishes to choose from.

- **Address**: Calle Cervantes, 8, 29016 Málaga, Spain.

Afternoon:

Spend your final afternoon at **Playa de Pedregalejo**, a quieter beach ideal for families. Stroll along the promenade, grab an ice cream, or simply relax by the sea.

- **Address**: Paseo Marítimo El Pedregal, 29017 Málaga, Spain.

This itinerary is perfect for families looking to explore **Malaga** *while keeping things fun, easy, and enjoyable for the kids. Make the most of your trip by taking in the sights, relaxing at the beach, and experiencing all that* **Malaga** *has to offer for families!*

PUENTE NUEVO

328 | MALAGA TRAVEL GUIDE 2025

Chapter 12

Useful Apps, Resources and Contacts

Navigating Málaga and the Costa del Sol is made easy with the right tools, resources, and contacts. Whether you're planning to explore historical landmarks, enjoy the beaches, or venture into nearby towns, having access to essential apps and reliable information ensures a smooth and enjoyable experience. This chapter highlights must-have apps, official contacts, emergency numbers, and trusted local guides to help you make the most of your trip.

Essential Travel Apps for Malaga

EMT Málaga App

If you're planning to use Málaga's public bus network, this app is a must. The **EMT Málaga App** provides real-time bus schedules, route maps, and nearby stops, making it easy to navigate the city without a car.

- **Website**: www.emtmalaga.es
- **Features**: Real-time bus updates, ticket purchase options, route planning, and nearby stops.
- **Tip**: Purchase a rechargeable bus card **(Tarjeta Transbordo)** for discounted fares and use the app to track your bus in real-time.

Visit Costa del Sol App

Created by Málaga's tourism board, this app is a comprehensive guide to the **Costa del Sol**. It features information about attractions, local events, dining options, and cultural activities throughout the region.

- **Website**: www.visitcostadelsol.com
- **Features**: Interactive maps, event calendars, itineraries, and recommendations for activities and dining.

- **Tip**: Use the **"hidden gems"** section to discover less-visited spots in Málaga and the surrounding areas.

Málaga Commuter Train App (Renfe Cercanías)

For those traveling to nearby towns like **Torremolinos, Fuengirola**, or **Benalmádena,** the **Renfe Cercanías app** provides train schedules, ticket purchasing options, and updates on commuter trains.

- **Website**: www.renfe.com
- **Features**: Real-time train schedules, notifications for delays, and route maps.
- **Tip**: Download your tickets in advance for hassle-free travel and use the app to check platform information.

Cabify

For quick and reliable transportation, **Cabify** is a ridesharing app widely used in Málaga. It's a convenient alternative to taxis and offers transparent pricing and cashless payments.

- **Website**: www.cabify.com
- **Features**: Ride-hailing, fare estimation, and multiple payment options.
- **Tip**: Use **Cabify** for airport transfers or late-night rides when public transport is less frequent.

Komoot

Komoot is perfect for exploring Málaga's natural beauty. This app is ideal for planning hikes, cycling routes, and walks along the coast or in nearby parks. It offers detailed maps and elevation profiles, ensuring a safe and enjoyable adventure.

Website: www.komoot.com

Features: GPS-enabled maps, user reviews, and offline route downloads.

Tip: Download your routes in advance for offline use, especially for trails like the **Caminito del Rey** or **Montes de Málaga**.

Google Maps

Google Maps remains a go-to app for navigation in Málaga. It provides detailed directions for driving, walking, cycling, and public transport, as well as recommendations for restaurants and attractions.

- **Website**: www.google.com/maps
- **Features**: Turn-by-turn navigation, saved locations, and offline maps.
- **Tip**: Save offline maps for areas with poor connectivity, like mountain trails or remote beaches.

Official Tourist Information and Visitor Contacts

Málaga Tourism Board

The **Málaga Tourism Board** operates several information centers in the city, offering free maps, brochures, and tailored advice. These centers are ideal for planning your activities, learning about local events, and receiving recommendations for attractions, transport, and eco-friendly travel.

- **Main Office Address**: Plaza de la Marina, 11, 29001 Málaga, Spain.
- **Website**: www.malagaturismo.com
- **Contact**: +34 951 92 60 20.
- **Opening Hours**: Daily, 9:00 AM – 7:00 PM.
- **Tip**: Ask about discounted tickets for museums, guided tours, and seasonal festivals.

Málaga Airport Tourist Office

Located in the arrivals hall, this office is your first stop for last-minute maps, public transport schedules, and tips for getting around the city. It's especially useful for travelers arriving in Málaga by air.

- **Address**: Málaga-Costa del Sol Airport, Terminal 3, 29004 Málaga, Spain.
- **Website**: www.aena.es
- **Contact**: +34 951 29 40 03.
- **Opening Hours**: Monday to Friday, 9:00 AM – 7:30 PM; Saturday and Sunday, 9:30 AM – 3:00 PM.
- **Tip**: The staff here can help you book airport transfers, taxis, or car rentals.

Regional Tourist Centers

In addition to Málaga city, there are tourist offices in nearby towns like **Nerja**, **Marbella**, and **Ronda**. These centers provide localized information on attractions, transport, and events specific to their areas.

- **Nerja Tourist Office Address**: Calle Carmen, 1, 29780 Nerja.
- **Contact**: +34 952 52 15 31.
- **Opening Hours**: Monday to Friday, 10:00 AM – 8:30 PM, Saturday and Sunday, 10:30 AM – 1:30 PM.

- **Marbella Tourist Office Address**: Plaza de los Naranjos, 29601 Marbella, Málaga, Spain.
- **Contact**: +34 952 765 04.

Emergency Contacts and Consular Services

Emergency Numbers

- **Police, Fire, and Ambulance**: 112 (EU-wide emergency number).
- **Local Police Málaga (Policía Local)**: +34 952 12 65 00.
- **Tourist Assistance Line**: +34 952 35 00 61.

Embassy and Consular Contacts

Having access to embassy and consulate information is essential when traveling, especially in case of emergencies such as lost documents, legal issues, or health concerns. Although Málaga doesn't have many full embassy offices, several honorary consulates operate in the city, and main embassies are located in Madrid.

United States Embassy

American citizens can contact the U.S. Embassy in Madrid for assistance with passport renewals, emergencies, and travel advice. Although there isn't a dedicated office in Málaga, they can provide support remotely.

- **Address**: Calle de Serrano, 75, 28006 Madrid, Spain.
- **Contact**: +34 915 87 22 00.

- **Opening Hours**: Monday to Friday, 8:30 AM – 5:30 PM (Closed on weekends and Spanish holidays).
- **Website**: https://es.usembassy.gov/
- **Tip**: Enroll in the **Smart Traveler Enrollment Program (STEP)** for travel updates and alerts.

British Consulate in Málaga

The British Consulate in Málaga provides assistance to UK nationals, including emergency travel documents, notarial services, and support in case of emergencies.

- **Address**: Edificio Eurocom, C. Mauricio Moro Pareto, 2, 29006 Málaga, Spain.
- **Contact**: +34 952 35 23 00.
- **Opening Hours**: 24-hour service.
- **Website**: https://www.gov.uk/world/organisations/british-consulate-malaga
- **Tip**: Contact the consulate in advance for appointments or to confirm required documents.

Canadian Consulate in Malaga

The Canadian Consulate in Málaga provides assistance to Canada nationals, including emergency travel documents, passport renewal, and support in case of emergencies.

- **Address**: Playa de la Malagueta, 2, Malaga-Este, 29016 Malaga, Spain.
- **Contact**: +34 952 22 33 46.
- **Tip**: For urgent issues, contact the Canadian Consulate in Barcelona.

German Honorary Consulate in Málaga

German citizens can access limited consular services in Málaga, such as passport assistance and guidance during emergencies.

- **Address**: Calle Mauricio Moro Pareto, 2, Distrito Centro, 29006 Malaga, Spain.
- **Contact**: +34 952 36 39 58.
- **Opening Hours:** Monday to Friday, 8:30 AM – 12:00PM (Closed on weekends and Spanish holidays).
- Website: https://spanien.diplo.de/es-de/
- **Tip**: For urgent issues, contact the German Embassy in Madrid.

Insider Tips for Consular Services

- Always carry a copy of your passport and travel insurance details.
- Some consulates require appointments for non-emergency services, so plan accordingly.

Local Guides and Tour Operators

Hiring a local guide or joining a trusted tour operator can help you discover Málaga's hidden gems and learn about its history and culture from a local perspective. Below are some trusted local guides and tour operators in Malaga:

Málaga Walks

Malagawalks offers small-group and private walking tours tailored to highlight Málaga's architectural and historical gems. Their guides are passionate about Málaga's heritage, ensuring you leave with a deeper understanding of the city.

- **Website**: www.malagawalks.com
- **Features**: Private tours, historic walks, and tapas tastings.
- **Tip**: Their sunset walking tour offers breathtaking views of the city and port.

Explora Málaga

This operator specializes in free walking tours and affordable guided experiences. Their enthusiastic guides bring Málaga's history to life with engaging storytelling and insider tips on the best places to eat, shop, and relax.

- **Website**: www.exploramalaga.com
- **Features**: Free walking tours, paid private tours, and family-friendly options.
- **Tip**: Take their guided **Alcazaba tour** for a detailed understanding of this historic Moorish fortress.

We Love Málaga

Offering personalized tours, *We Love Málaga* caters to travelers who want a deeper understanding of the city's culture and heritage.

- **Website**: www.welovemalaga.com
- **Features**: Custom private tours, day trips to nearby towns, and gastronomy experiences.
- **Tip**: Try their private **Picasso-themed tour** to learn about Málaga's most famous artist while exploring key landmarks tied to his life.

Málaga Adventures

Málaga Adventures specializes in small-group walking tours that explore the city's rich history and culture. Their passionate guides offer tours covering Málaga's highlights, including the **Alcazaba, Roman Theatre**, and **Málaga Cathedral**, as well as more specialized tours like tapas tastings and street art explorations.

- **Website**: www.malagaadventures.com
- **Features**: Free walking tours, private city tours, tapas tours, and day trips.
- **Tip**: Join their morning walking tour to avoid the midday heat and explore **Málaga's Old Town** in a relaxed atmosphere.

Costa Excursions

Costa Excursions provides private day trips and transportation services to popular destinations around Málaga. Whether you want to visit the whitewashed villages of **Mijas**, the historic town of **Ronda**, or the stunning **Caminito del Rey**, *Costa Excursions* creates personalized itineraries tailored to your preferences.

- **Website**: www.costaexcursions.es
- **Features**: Private transportation, customizable day trips, and group excursions.
- **Tip**: Their **"Highlights of Ronda and Setenil"** tour is highly recommended for its combination of history and natural beauty.

Málaga Bike Tours by Kay Farrell

For an active and eco-friendly way to explore Málaga, Málaga Bike Tours offers guided bike rides through the city's historic streets, beaches, and parks. Their knowledgeable guides share local stories and interesting facts, making the experience both fun and informative.

- **Website**: www.malagabiketours.eu
- **Features**: City bike tours, sunset rides, and beach tours.
- **Tip**: Book their family-friendly bike tour, which includes plenty of stops for kids to rest and enjoy the sights.

By equipping yourself with these apps, resources, and contacts, you'll have all the tools you need for a seamless and enriching visit to Málaga. Whether exploring the city's culture or adventuring into the Costa del Sol, these tools will enhance your experience.

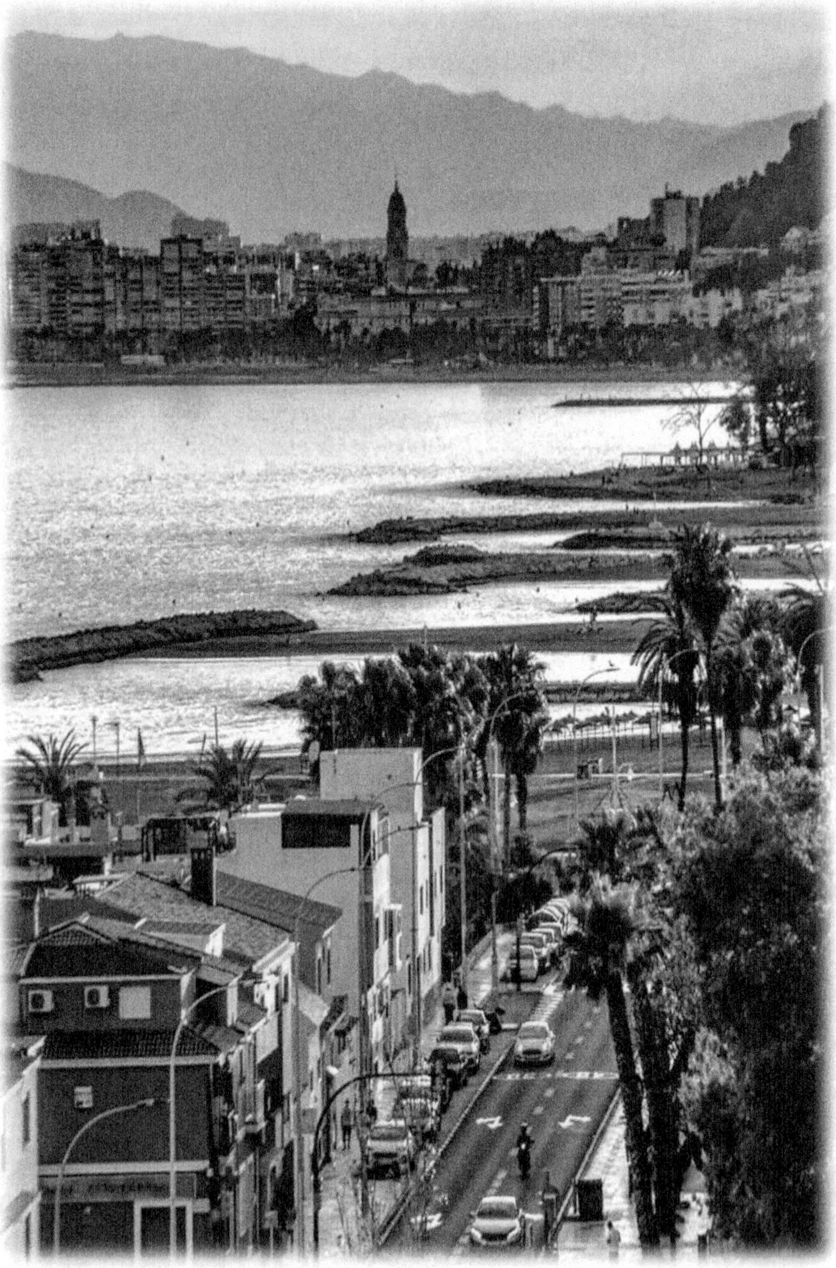

Conclusion

As we reach the final pages of this guide, it's clear that Málaga is not just a place you visit—it's a destination that welcomes you like an old friend, with open arms and stories to share. From its sun-drenched beaches to its ancient streets steeped in history, Málaga invites you to slow down, savor every moment, and immerse yourself in its rhythm. It's a city that leaves its mark on your heart, long after your journey ends.

Walking through Málaga isn't just about seeing its iconic landmarks—it's about feeling the echoes of history as you wander the **Alcazaba**, marveling at the enduring beauty of the **Roman Theatre**, and discovering the quiet strength of the **Gibralfaro Castle** as it watches over the city. It's about tasting the soul of **Andalusia** in a dish of freshly grilled sardines at a **chiringuito** or in the complex sweetness of a local Málaga wine.

But what truly makes Málaga unforgettable is the warmth of its people. It's the smile of the shopkeeper at **the Atarazanas Market** who offers you a taste of their finest olives, the laughter shared over tapas at a family-run restaurant, or the stories told by a local guide as they bring the city's history to life. Málaga isn't just a city you explore—it's a place you connect with.

As you reflect on your time here, remember that every moment—whether you were soaking in the sunset from **Playa de la Malagueta**, wandering the cobbled streets of **the Old Town**, or savoring the quiet beauty of the **Montes de Málaga**—was part of a greater experience. An experience that goes beyond sights and sounds, one that lingers in your soul and reminds you why we travel in the first place.

Traveling to Málaga is about more than checking destinations off a list—it's about being present in the moment, embracing new experiences, and letting a place change you in ways you didn't expect.

Málaga is a city you can visit over and over again, each time discovering something new, each time finding a deeper appreciation for its layers of history, culture, and natural beauty. And whether this is your first visit or one of many, know that Málaga will always have more to offer—its doors are always open, its sunsets always golden, its streets always ready to share another story.

Thank you for allowing this guide to accompany you on your journey. May Málaga inspire you, fill you with wonder, and remind you of the beauty of exploration. Safe travels, and may the memories of Málaga stay with you, long after you've left its shores.
Until next time, Hasta luego!

TRAVEL PLANNER

TRAVEL PLANNER BONUS

345 | MALAGA TRAVEL GUIDE 2025

TRAVEL

DATE:
DURATION:

DESTINATION:

PLACES TO SEE:
1. _____
2. _____
3. _____
4. _____
5. _____
6. _____
7. _____

LOCAL FOOD TO TRY:
1. _____
2. _____
3. _____
4. _____
5. _____
6. _____
7. _____

DAY 1

DAY 2

DAY 3

DAY 4

DAY 5

DAY 6

NOTES

EXPENSES IN TOTAL:

PLANNER

TRAVEL

DATE:
DURATION:

DESTINATION:

PLACES TO SEE:
1. _____
2. _____
3. _____
4. _____
5. _____
6. _____
7. _____

LOCAL FOOD TO TRY:
1. _____
2. _____
3. _____
4. _____
5. _____
6. _____
7. _____

DAY 1	DAY 2	DAY 3

DAY 4	DAY 5	DAY 6

NOTES

EXPENSES IN TOTAL:

PLANNER

TRAVEL

DATE:
DURATION:

DESTINATION:

PLACES TO SEE:
1. _____
2. _____
3. _____
4. _____
5. _____
6. _____
7. _____

LOCAL FOOD TO TRY:
1. _____
2. _____
3. _____
4. _____
5. _____
6. _____
7. _____

DAY 1	DAY 2	DAY 3

DAY 4	DAY 5	DAY 6

NOTES

EXPENSES IN TOTAL:

PLANNER

TRAVEL

DATE:
DURATION:

DESTINATION:

PLACES TO SEE:
1.
2.
3.
4.
5.
6.
7.

LOCAL FOOD TO TRY:
1.
2.
3.
4.
5.
6.
7.

DAY 1	DAY 2	DAY 3

DAY 4	DAY 5	DAY 6

NOTES

EXPENSES IN TOTAL:

PLANNER

TRAVEL

DATE:
DURATION:

DESTINATION:

PLACES TO SEE:
1.
2.
3.
4.
5.
6.
7.

LOCAL FOOD TO TRY:
1.
2.
3.
4.
5.
6.
7.

DAY 1	DAY 2	DAY 3

DAY 4	DAY 5	DAY 6

NOTES

EXPENSES IN TOTAL:

PLANNER

Printed in Great Britain
by Amazon